Paul

Women

and

Church

****

Eddie L. Hyatt

Foreword by Susan Stubbs Hyatt

****

HYATT PRESS * 2016

*Publish, and set up a standard; publish
and conceal not* (Jeremiah 50:2)

PAUL, WOMEN & CHURCH
By Eddie L. Hyatt

© 2016 by Hyatt International Ministries, Incorporated

Published by Hyatt Press
A Subsidiary of Hyatt Int'l Ministries, Incorporated

Mailing Address (2016)
P. O. Box 3877
Grapevine, TX 76099-3877

Internet Addresses
Email: dreddiehyatt@gmail.com
Web Site: www.eddiehyatt.com
Social Media: Eddie L. Hyatt

Cover and Book Design by Susan C. Hyatt

Unless otherwise indicated, all Scripture quotations
are taken from the New Kings James Version of the Bible. ©
1979, 1980, 1982 by Thomas Nelson, Inc. Publishers.

ISBN: 978-1-888435-56-6

Printed in the United States of America

About the Author

Dr. Eddie L. Hyatt is a seasoned minister of the Gospel with over 40 years of ministerial experience as a pastor, Bible teacher, and Professor of Theology. He holds the Doctor of Ministry from Regent University, as well as the Master of Divinity and a Master of Arts degrees from Oral Roberts University. He did post-graduate studies at the Center for Advanced Theological Studies at Fuller Theological Seminary. Dr. Hyatt has lectured on revival, Church history, and various Biblical themes in churches, conferences, and some of the major educational institutions in the world, including Christ Church Oxford University, Doulos Bible College in India, Oral Roberts University, Zion Bible College, and Christ for the Nations Institute. He has authored several books, including *2000 Years of Charismatic Christianity*, which is used as a textbook in colleges and seminaries around the world. Eddie's passion is to see God's people learn to "think Biblically" and to see authentic Spiritual awakening transform the Church and impact the world in the 21st century.

Contact Information. If you would like to correspond with Eddie for any reason, including invitations to speak, you may do so at any of the following:

Email: dreddiehyatt@gmail.com
Website: www.eddiehyatt.com
Social Media: Eddie L. Hyatt
Mailing Address: P. O. Box 3877, Grapevine TX 76099

Contents

Foreword

"God, why do you hate me?" asked a young lady when she read the translation of Paul's words in I Timothy 2:11-12. A new believer from Romania, she was studying the New Testament after having recently accepting Jesus as her Savior and Lord. And when she arrived at Paul's writings, she was stunned by what he seemed to be saying about her, as a woman. It was so different from the acceptance and joy that faith in the Lord Jesus had given her. She was confused and demoralized.

Thank God! She was enrolled in one of Eddie's courses in Bible college and heard the truth. The truth that you will read in this book witnessed with her heart and revived the Life of the Spirit in her inner being. No more confusion!

Whether we are willing to acknowledge it or not, this woman's experience of suppression and subordination is repeated in the lives of most Christian women, with varying degrees of intensity. That is to say, what we experience "in the Spirit" is so opposite to what we are told that the Bible says about us as women.

This is the fault of ill-informed Church leaders who willingly take Paul's writings out of context and impose ideas opposite to what Paul himself believed, lived, and taught. It is the fault of traditional translation and interpretation informed by the pagan thesis that women are evil, inferior, unequal, and unclean.

Contrary to this is the Biblical thesis that men and women are equal in terms of substance and value, privilege and responsibility, function and authority, in all areas of life and leadership, ministry and marriage. This is what Jesus taught, what Creation teaches, and what the Holy Spirit has taught throughout Church history, both individually in the hearts of true Believers, and corporately through Holy Spirit revivals. It is also what Paul teaches in His Epistles, correctly understood.

Now, Eddie has extended and deepened my own Biblical, theological, and historical research in this area, strengthening our understanding of the Biblical truth. I am thrilled! Like me, he has been willing to risk rejection, slander, and misunderstanding to proclaim the Gospel in all of its fullness for the sake of God's people and His Kingdom.

Eddie first developed the material in this book in a 10-lesson course by the same name. From the beginning, it was clear that he needed to capture his findings in book form, and now he has done this. I know the good fruit will be abundant and will remain, setting free the captives from traditional lies propagated by an ill-informed Church and various socio-religious cultures.

This book comes at a critical time in history. From the time of the Reformation, beginning with Martin Luther's proclamation of the doctrine of the priesthood of all believers, a gradual Restoration of the Biblical Message and the Gospel of Jesus Christ has been occurring. After centuries in the Dark Middle Ages, the Reformation brought Light by putting the Bible in the hands of the masses, with leaders like Martin Luther (1483-1546) and George Fox (1624-1691) introducing a social model in which both girls and boys were educated and taught to read so that they could gain knowledge of Scripture and develop Biblical lifestyles. Scripture in the hands of Believers gave the Holy Spirit substance with which to work, and from that beginning of Reform, have come Revivals, each of which has Restored a strategic Biblical, Gospel doctrine.

Now is the time that God, through informed study of Scripture and the ministry of the Holy Spirit by highly educated Believers, is restoring the truth of Biblical equality. We are honored to do our small—but strategic – part in God's Big Plan.

As you read this important Bible study, allow the Holy Spirit to birth a greater sense of personal responsibility in you and to awaken new hope in your spirit and soul to fulfil your reason for His having given you both life and New Life. As you do this, men will find freedom from the ungodly load of responsibility imposed on them by unbiblical teaching, while women will find new freedom to walk out God's will and purpose. You will discover the joy of functioning, not on the basis of gender roles defined by fallen, religious culture, but rather, according to the leading of the Holy Spirit in accordance with your natural and spiritual giftings; your unique God-given personalities; and your eternally important, God-ordained purpose and commissioning.

If you are truly serious about being a Disciple of Our Lord Jesus Christ, this book is for you.

Susan Stubbs Hyatt, D.Min.,
MA, MA, BCA, Cert. Life Coach, Lic. Teacher.
President/CEO, God's Word to Women, Inc.
Grapevine, Texas, USA

Preface

If a person's importance is measured not by likeability but by his or her influence on the course of human history, then Saul of Tarsus deserves all the energy we can expend to get a fix on who he was, what made him tick and why he did the things he did.

Professor Ben Witherington III

When it comes to the topic of women and church, no one has been misunderstood and misjudged more than Paul. Castigated as a misogynist and woman-hater by some, he has been the particular target for barbs and insults from liberal theologians, secularists and those with a bias against Christianity.

For example, one popular feminist "reconstruction" of Christian origins, contains an imaginary epistle written to the churches by Phoebe, a woman leader whom Paul mentions and affirms in Romans 16:1-2. In this fantasy letter, Phoebe expresses concern that Paul has become preoccupied with "putting women back in their proper place" and concludes it is because he is "so taken up with giving a good impression to the pagans."[1]

In the same vein of prejudicial animosity toward Paul, another liberal writer has blatantly declared,

> Paul, sacred apostle of Christ, was an ignorant misogynist in many respects, and any man who follows in his footsteps treads down a dangerous path.[2]

9

On other end of the spectrum, fundamentalists and evangelical Christians respect Paul, but use his writings to marginalize women and confine them to subservient roles in the church and the home. They too misunderstand Paul and misinterpret his writings, but from a different paradigm and point of view. Both liberals and fundamentalists do a disservice to the body of Christ and the mission of the church because both misunderstand and misinterpret Paul.

My goal in writing this book is to rehabilitate Paul's reputation in this regard and show that he was, in fact, a friend of women and a champion for their freedom in Christ. I will show that he considered this a part of his call to preach the gospel of Christ to the Gentile world. This gospel message included the good news of the emancipation of women through the death and resurrection of Jesus Christ.

Paul was a committed disciple of Christ and God's chosen instrument to take the message of Jesus' life, death and resurrection, that occurred in a Jewish cultural milieu, to the Gentile world and interpret it for a Roman/Hellenistic audience. His letters represent his efforts to convey the message of Jesus to various Gentile cultures of the ancient, Greco-Roman world, which is why they can be so challenging to comprehend.

If you have grappled with understanding Paul's writings, consider yourself in good company. Simon Peter also grappled with understanding Paul's letters. In II Peter 3:14-

16, Peter affirmed the writings of Paul to his audience and referred to them as "Scripture." He wrote,

> *And consider that the longsuffering of our Lord is salvation—as also our beloved brother Paul, according to the wisdom given to him, has written to you, as also in all his epistles, speaking in them of things, in which are some things hard to understand, which untaught and unstable people twist to their own destruction, as they do also the rest of the Scriptures* (II Peter 3:15-16).

Although liberal scholars do not consider II Peter to be an authentic letter, we embrace a more conservative view of Scripture, which assumes that all the books of the New Testament canon were written by the traditional authors. We, therefore, approach all the traditional letters of Paul, including the Pastorals, as genuine and authentic.

In the above passage, Peter says that many in his day were twisting Paul's writings to their own destruction. That twisting continues today, particularly in regards to what Paul wrote about women. Our goal is not to write a commentary on Paul's writings about women, but to show Paul himself in a new light as a friend of women and a champion of their equality in Christ.

Chapter I

Paul: The Man, The Message & The Mission

But when it pleased God, who separated me from my mother's
womb and called me through His grace, to reveal His Son in me,
that I might preach Him among the Gentiles.
Paul, Galatians 1:15-16

Paul was uniquely and providentially prepared for his heavenly assignment to be the apostle to the Gentiles, taking the Good News of Jesus Christ to the men and women of the Greco-Roman world. Such an assignment required a unique individual; one comfortable with Gentile ways and culture while at the same time totally committed to the God of Israel and the Old Testament Scriptures. This one must be able to move and discourse with both Jewish and pagan traditions and at the same time challenge those traditions with the gospel message and its new status for women.

Greek & Roman Influences in Paul

These criteria were all found in Paul. He was born in Tarsus and was a citizen of that city. Tarsus was located in present day Turkey about twelve miles inland from the

Mediterranean Sea and 356 miles north of Jerusalem. Tarsus was, in Paul's words, *no mean city* (Acts 21:39), meaning "no insignificant city."

Tarsus was profoundly influenced by the Greek language and culture, and its philosophical schools rivalled those of Athens and Alexandria. It was also a busy commercial center and capital of the Roman province of Cilicia. Today, the population of Tarsus is around 3 million.

Growing up in the city of Tarsus (as well as Jerusalem) meant that Paul was conversant in Greek and familiar with Greek/Gentile ways and customs. Being a philosophical center, Paul would have been exposed to Greek philosophy and thinking.

Paul was also a Roman citizen, having inherited Roman citizenship from his father, which meant he would have enjoyed a certain elite status in the city of Tarsus. This also meant that he would also have been familiar with the Roman legal system.

His Jewish Upbringing

In spite of the Greek and Roman influences, Paul's parents were Jews who strictly adhered to the Jewish laws and customs. The evidence indicates that both Paul and his father (or an ancestor) were Pharisees for Paul said of himself before the Sanhedrin, *I am a Pharisee, the son of a Pharisee* (Acts 23:6).

The word Pharisee means "separated one" and the sect arose around 200 B.C. as a defense against Greek ways and customs that were infiltrating the Jews and their way of life. Although their reason for being was admirable, they became very legalistic and self-righteous as we learn from the gospels.

At an early age, Paul was sent to Jerusalem to be educated in the school of Gamaliel, the most famous rabbi and Pharisee of the day (Acts 22:3). Paul's description of himself as *a Hebrew of Hebrews* (Phil. 3:5) is precise language, probably indicating that Hebrew was the language of both the home and the synagogue he and his family attended.

As Paul matured, he became very zealous for Jewish laws and tradition. He also became well known for his advanced learning and intense religious fervor. His rabbinic and Pharisaical training became the fuel that drove him to become a zealous persecutor of the followers of Jesus.

The Scandal of a Crucified Messiah

Paul, like most of Israel, anticipated the coming of the promised Messiah (I Sam. 7:12-13; Isaiah 9:6-7). They were, however, looking for a political and militaristic Messiah who would defeat the Romans, restore the national and political fortunes of Israel and make her, once again, a nation to be reckoned with in the earth.

Paul, therefore, became enraged at the claims of the followers of Jesus that He was Israel's Messiah — a Messiah who had been crucified by the Romans, raised from the dead and had ascended into heaven. For Paul, the message of a crucified Messiah was a contradiction in terms and abhorrent. A crucified individual was the epitome of weakness, suffering and shame, the very antithesis of what the first-century Jew looked for in their promised Messiah.

Furthermore, the Scripture had said, *He who is hanged on a tree is accursed of God* (Deut. 21:23). For Paul and many other Jewish leaders, everything that was of value in Judaism was being imperiled by the preaching and activities of the followers of Jesus. As far he was concerned, those who preached such an abhorrent message as a crucified Messiah were deserving of imprisonment and death.

Paul Becomes the Chief Persecutor of Christians

This is why he participated in the death of Stephen, guarding the garments of those who actually carried out the stoning (Acts 22:19-20). From there, Paul began spearheading a systematic persecution of the followers of Jesus aiming to wipe out this new Messianic movement.

In Acts 26:11 Paul describes his anger and hate for the followers of Jesus at this time. He said, *And I punished them in every synagogue and compelled them to blaspheme; and being exceedingly enraged against them, I persecuted them even to foreign cities.*

Acts 9:1-2 says that Paul obtained letters of authorization from the high priest, *so that if he found any who were of the Way,* **whether men or women**, *he might bring them to Jerusalem.* The fact that Paul requested authorization to arrest both men and women demonstrates the prominent role women were having at this early stage. Paul knew that if he had any chance of stopping this Messianic movement, he would have to target the women as well as the men.

Paul Encounters the Risen Messiah

While on his way to Damascus to arrest followers of Jesus, Paul had an experience that radically changed and altered him for the rest of his life (Acts 9:1-19). As he neared Damascus, a bright light from heaven suddenly shone around him and blinded him. He fell to the ground and heard a voice saying, *Saul, Saul why are you persecuting Me?*

The Person speaking revealed Himself as Jesus. Paul was stunned! The Jesus He so hated was really alive. The message he was trying to stamp out was true. We can only imagine the mental and emotional trauma of that moment as he lay in the dust of the Damascus Road having encountered the risen Lord. His entire world was suddenly upended.

The voice then instructed Paul to go to a particular house on a particular street and await further instructions. In the meantime, God spoke to a disciple named Ananias to go and lay his hand on Paul and speak certain words to him. Ananias obeyed and Luke says, *Immediately, there fell from his eyes something like scales, and he received his sight at once; and he arose and was baptized* (Acts 9:18).

A New Paradigm & Purpose for Paul

As a Pharisee, the Law had been the center of Paul's life. But now a Person—Jesus Christ—becomes the center of his life, and all the Old Testament Scriptures are now seen in a new light and within a new paradigm (see Romans 10:1-4). He immediately began to preach in the synagogues that Jesus is the Messiah to the amazement of everyone. Luke says,

16

Immediately he preached the Christ in the synagogues, that He is the Son of God. Then all who heard were amazed and said, "Is this not he who destroyed those who called on this name in Jerusalem, and has come here for that purpose, so that he might bring them to the high priest? But Saul increased all the more in strength, and confounded the Jews who dwelt in Damascus, proving that Jesus is the Christ (Messiah). (Acts 9:20-23).

Suffering the Loss of All Things

When the Lord instructed Ananias to go and lay his hands on Saul, He had said to him, *For I will show him how many things he must suffer for My name's sake* (Acts 915-16). This suffering for the Lord's name began almost immediately for Paul.

The Jews in Damascus became so infuriated that Paul was now preaching the gospel he once sought to destroy, that they plotted to kill him. He escaped when some of the disciples in Damascus let him down over the city wall in a basket at night.

He then travelled to Jerusalem and sought to join himself with the disciples there, but they were all afraid of him. They obviously doubted the story of his conversion. Barnabas, however, took Paul and brought him to the apostles and told them of his incredible encounter with the risen Lord on the Damascus road.

He was then accepted into their company and began speaking boldly in the name of Jesus in Jerusalem, especially to the Greek-speaking Jews (Acts 9:29). They too became enraged and plotted to kill Paul. When the believers in Jerusalem learned of this plot, they helped him on his way to Caesarea and then to his hometown of Tarsus, where we have to assume he was reunited with family, kinfolk, and longtime acquaintances.

How did his parents and kinfolk receive his testimony of having become a follower of Jesus Christ? The evidence suggests that they rejected Paul and disowned him. He never mentions them in his letters, but in his letter to the Philippians he refers to his commitment to Jesus Christ and then says, *For whom I have suffered the loss of all things* (Philippians 3:8).

Sometime later, Barnabas came to Tarsus in search of Paul. He found him and brought him to Antioch in Syria where there was a thriving Christian community, comprised mostly of Gentile followers of Jesus. In fact, Luke notes that it was in Antioch that the disciples of Jesus were first called "Christians" (Acts 11:26).

Paul seemed to fit well with these Gentile followers of Jesus and Antioch, for a time, became his base of operations. It was from Antioch that he began the missionary journeys that would change the course of world history.

It was in these missionary journeys that he established congregations to whom he would later write letters of instruction and encouragement. It was also in these journeys that he met and became the friend of many women who became, in his own words, his coworkers.

And the women who had come with Him from Galilee followed after, and they observed the tomb and how His body was laid (Luke 23:55).

Now on the first day of the week, very early in the morning they, and certain other women with them, came to the tomb bringing the spices which they had prepared (Luke 24:1-2).

Then they returned from the tomb and told all these things to the eleven and to all the rest. It was Mary Magdalene, Joanna, Mary the mother of James, and the other women with them . . . (Luke24:10).

Now when He rose early on the first day of the week, He appeared first to Mary Magdalene, out of whom He had cast seven demons. She went and told those who had been with Him, as they mourned and wept (Mark 16:9-11).

These all continued with one accord in prayer and supplication, with the women and Mary the mother of Jesus, and with His brothers (Acts 1:13-14).

Many of these women had followed Jesus to Jerusalem from Galilee. They had left everything to follow Him. They were totally committed to Him.

They observed his crucifixion and wept. The also made a point to observe where his body was laid so they could bring spices and show honor to Him in his death. They were the last ones to leave the cross and the first ones at his tomb on resurrection morning. They were also the first to be honored with an appearance from their risen Lord.

It is, therefore, no stretch of the imagination to envision these women as among the most committed and passionate of Jesus' followers. They had already broken social and cultural traditions by leaving their homes and families to follow Him. They had already put their lives at risk to identify with Him in His arrest and crucifixion. Now that they know He has risen from the dead, no power on earth can keep them from proclaiming the good news.

It is, therefore, no wonder that Saul the Pharisee targeted the women followers of Jesus for persecution and imprisonment. They were obviously playing very prominent roles in the spread of this early Messianic movement.

Paul, therefore, even before his conversion was aware of the prominent role women played in the spread of early Christianity. Then, after his conversion, Paul had many positive relationships with women as friends and coworkers. One he recognized as an apostle, another served in a leadership role toward him, another was a close friend, and another was a spiritual mother to him.

A Female Apostle

In his letter to the church at Rome, Paul sends personal greetings to twenty-four people in the latter part of the letter, *i.e.*, chapter sixteen. These individuals are friends and coworkers who are dear to his heart. Of the twenty-four mentioned by name, ten are women. Many of these obviously functioned in roles of leadership in the churches.

One woman named Junia is specifically referred to as an apostle. In Rom. 16:7 Paul says, *Greet Andronicus and Junia, my countrymen and my fellow prisoners, who are of note among the apostles who also were in Christ before me.*

Junia is a feminine name and was universally recognized as a female apostle for the first several centuries of the Church's existence. The famous church father of the fifth century, John Chrysostom, exclaimed, "Oh how great is the devotion of this woman, that she should be even counted worthy of the appellation of apostle."[3]

Concerned by the presence of a female apostle, some have attempted to argue that the name should be translated "Junias," which is male. There are insurmountable facts, however, that militate against this argument.

First of all, without exception, all ancient Greek manuscripts have the feminine form of Junia, not Junias. Secondly, the female name Junia was quite common in the first century whereas the male name, Junias, is unknown. Junias, therefore, is a hypothetical name. Thirdly, as mentioned above, Junia was universally recognized as a female apostle for the first several centuries of the Church's existence.

Why then have some modern translations, such as the 1984 NIV, rendered the name Junias instead of Junia? Dr. N. Clayton Croy, Professor of New Testament at Trinity Lutheran Seminary in Columbus, Ohio, says, "It is hard to see any reason other than the translators' bias against the possibility that a woman could be an apostle." [4] Well-known New Testament scholar, James G. D. Dunn, says, "The assumption that the name must be male is a striking indictment of male presumption regarding the character and structure of earliest Christianity." [5]

The evidence is conclusive that Junia was a female apostle and recognized as such by Paul himself. The evidence is so conclusive, in fact, that the 2011 edition of the NIV has replaced the word "Junias" with "Junia."

Paul's recognition of Junia as an apostle clearly demonstrates that he was no misogynist and that women exercised leadership roles in the New Testament churches. But she is not alone, for a careful perusal of Scripture reveals other women who functioned in leadership roles in the New Testament.

A Woman Minister Respected by Paul

Phoebe was a woman for whom Paul had great respect as is borne out in the language he used to describe her. The power of his words is lost in our English translations, but is very obvious in the Greek (Romans 16:1-2).

In Romans 16:1, Paul refers to Phoebe as *a servant of the church in Cenchrea*. "The word "servant" in this passage is misleading. It is from the Greek word *diakonos* and should be translated as "minister." Indeed, *diakonos* is translated as "minister" in twenty-three places where it is used of men, including Paul, Barnabas, and Apollos (I Corinthians 3:4). In this one place where it is used of a woman, these same translators chose to use the word "servant," a clear example of their bias.

Diakonos does literally means "servant" but became a word for Christian leaders as a result of Jesus using it in response to the request by James and John for special seats of power in His kingdom. Jesus replied that whoever wanted to be great must become a *diakonos,* or "servant." From that declaration of Jesus, *diakonos* became a common designation for Christian ministers, highlighting the servant character of Christian leadership. The well-known evangelical theologian, E. Earle Ellis, wrote,

> *Diakonos* is used frequently in the Pauline letters for those who exercise ministries of teaching and preaching. The title is given to Paul and to a number of his associates who are active on a continuing basis as traveling missionaries or as coworkers in local congregations. In terms of modern function, it best corresponds to the modern designation "minister."

Designating Phoebe as a *diakonos* shows that she was a "minister" from the church in Cenchrea who had been sent by that church to Rome on a special assignment. Paul recognizes her as such by using the same word for her that he uses for himself, for Barnabas, and for Apollos.

Paul also said that Phoebe had been a *prostatis* to many, *and of myself also.* The KJV and NKJV translate the word as "helper," but *Thayer's Greek-English Lexicon* says that *prostatis* refers to "a woman set over others" and that it describes Phoebe as a "guardian, protector, and benefactor." *Vine's Expository Dictionary of New Testament Words* says that *prostatis* is a word of "dignity" and indicates the high esteem with which she was regarded.

These definitions are correct for *prostatis* is made up of the prefix *pro*, meaning "before," and *"istemi,"* meaning "to stand." It, therefore, literally means "to stand before" and identifies Phoebe as a leader with the qualities one would expect in a modern day pastor.

Some will argue that Phoebe was merely a patroness to Paul who supplied financial support for his ministry. However, the overall sense of the passage, including Paul's designation of her as a "minister," militates against such an interpretation. She was one who had "stood before" others, including Paul himself.

An argument could be made from this passage that Phoebe had, at some time, functioned in a pastoral type role toward Paul. She is obviously held in very high esteem by him for he exhorts the Roman believers, both men and women, to receive her and respect her *in the Lord in a manner worthy of the saints*, and to assist her *in whatever business she has need of you* (Romans 16:2).

Priscilla: A Pastor and Close Friend

In Roman 16:3-5 Paul greets Priscilla and her husband Aquilla, whom he always mentions together. They obviously functioned in a mutual partnership, for not only does Paul always mention them together, he always uses the plural pronouns, "they" and "them," when referring to them. In vs. 5, for example, he sends greetings to "them" and to the church that is in "their" house.

It is likely that Priscilla was the out-front one in their ministry and the pastor of the church in their house. This is indicated by the fact that when referring to them, Paul mentions Priscilla first. This goes against the proper, conventional practice in the ancient world of always mentioning the man first. That Paul would mention Priscilla first is a powerful statement of her status and influence, and of Paul's estimation of her.

Paul first met this couple when he went to Corinth to preach the gospel. They welcomed him into their home and he worked with them in their tent-making business, the vocation in which Paul had also been trained. They were Jewish followers of Jesus as was Paul. The three of them had much in common and became very close friends (Acts 18:1-3).

When Paul departed Corinth, Priscilla and Aquilla departed with him but they remained in Ephesus and hosted a congregation in their home while Paul went on to Jerusalem and Antioch. Paul later returned to Ephesus and reconnected with this couple. When he wrote his first letter to Corinth from Ephesus he included greetings from Priscilla and Aquilla *and the church that is in their house* (I Corinthians 16:19).

In his letter to the Romans, Paul sends greetings to Priscilla and Aquilla who were in Rome preaching the gospel and hosting a church in their home (Romans 16:3-5). In vs. 4 he says that they *risked their necks for my life*. Sometime before this, perhaps during the eighteen months they were together in Corinth, Priscilla and Aquilla had put their lives at risk for Paul, for which he publicly thanked them. Paul's estimation of this couple and their influence is shown in his words, *to whom not only I give thanks, but also all the churches of the Gentiles.* (Romans 16:4). Priscilla was a woman leader recognized and respected by Paul.

Paul's "Spiritual Mother"

In Romans 16:13 Paul sends greetings to Rufus, *and his mother and mine.* This is obviously not Paul's biological mother, but is a woman who has been a spiritual mother to him. We know little about this woman but at some point in Paul's spiritual journey she had offered encouragement and counsel to Paul and been like a mother to him.

The identity of this woman can perhaps be identified by comparing Paul's words in this passage to Mark's gospel, which also mentions an individual named Rufus. Since Paul's letter and Mark's gospel were both written to the same Christian community in Rome, and within a few years of each other, it is likely that the Rufus mentioned by Paul and the Rufus mentioned by Mark are the same person.

In his gospel, which was originally written to the church in Rome, Mark tells of Simon of Cyrene being compelled to carry the cross of Jesus (Mark 15:21). He mentions that Simon was the father of *Alexander and Rufus* and the way he presents these two names indicates that Alexander and Rufus were well known to the Christians in Rome.

Mark obviously expects his audience to make the connection when they read that Simon of Cyrene is the father of these two individuals who are part of their community. The Rufus of Paul, therefore, is most likely the Rufus of Mark, the son of Simon of Cyrene who carried the cross of Jesus.

Paul never mentions a spiritual father in his writings, but he does make a point to send greetings to his spiritual mother. His spiritual mother was likely an African woman from Cyrene (Cyrene is located on the north coast of Africa), the mother of Rufus and the wife of Simon of Cyrene who carried the cross of Jesus.

Paul Was No Misogynist

There are many more women in Paul's life such as those in Philippi whom he said *labored with me in the gospel* (Philippians 4:3) and the numerous women he greets in the last chapter of Romans including the ones whom he says had also "labored" with him in the gospel.

Yes, it is obvious that Paul was no misogynist. Even a cursory reading of the New Testament with an open mind will reveal a Paul who was very open and accepting towards women and their gifts. This is why the noted New Testament scholar, F. F. Bruce, wrote,

> He [Paul] delighted in the company of his fellows, both men and women. The most incredible feature in the Paul of popular mythology is his alleged misogyny. He treated women as persons. The mainstream churches of Christendom, as they inch along towards a worthier recognition of the ministry of women, have some way to go yet before they come abreast of Paul.

Chapter 3

Paul & the God-Fearing Women of Philippi

*And on the Sabbath day we went out of the city
to the riverside, where prayer was customarily made;
and we sat down and spoke to the women who met there..*

Acts 16:13-15

Paul had no problem working and building with women. In fact, he began the first church in Europe with women and its first meeting place was in the home of a woman. In recounting the founding of the church in Philippi, Luke says;

> *And on the Sabbath day we went out of the city to the riverside, where prayer was customarily made; and we sat down and spoke to the women who met there* (Acts 16:13).

Paul first visited Philippi probably in the year A.D. 50 during his second missionary journey, accompanied by Luke, Silas, and Timothy. They were in the coastal city of Troas when Paul had a night vision (Acts 16:9) in which he saw a man of Macedonia saying, *Come over into Macedonia and help us.* Based on the vision they travelled to Philippi, a leading city of Macedonia, situated on the main highway that connected the eastern provinces of the Roman Empire with Rome.

Founded by Philip of Macedon, the father of Alexander the Great, in 358-57 B.C., it was a pagan city filled with much occultic activity and idolatry. This is the first time on record of the gospel being preached in Europe.

Paul Begins with Women

Paul always began his ministry in the local synagogues because, as a Pharisee and teacher of Judaism, he always had an opening there. The synagogues were made up of three kinds of people; (1) Jews, (2) Proselytes, (Gentile converts to Judaism), and (3) God-fearers (those Gentiles who were attracted to the Jewish message of the one true God but were not ready to obligate themselves to the Jewish Law).

The Jewish community in Philippi was obviously small since there was no synagogue. A quorum of ten Jewish men, who were heads of households, was required for establishing a synagogue in any community. In Philippi there was only a place of prayer by the river where some women met on a regular basis.

Because there was no synagogue, these women, probably Jews and Gentile God-fearers, were meeting for prayer by the river each Sabbath. Paul thus began the church in Philippi with a group of God-fearing women who were meeting together on a regular basis for prayer.

Notice that Paul did not search the city for property where he could put up a "church" building, nor did he do a demographic study and survey as to where in the city to establish a "church." Nor did he say, "We have to first find some men." He went where there were open and hungry hearts. Jewish tradition might require ten men to open a synagogue, but Paul was very comfortable beginning a Christian congregation with a group of praying women.

Notice Paul's very personal and compassionate approach to the women who were meeting by the river for prayer. Luke says, *And we sat down and spoke to the women who met there* (Acts 16:13). Paul did not "preach" to them, nor did he invite them to a meeting. He sat down, looked then in the eye and conversed with them.

He got to know these women and allowed them to know him. No wonder the British, New Testament scholar, F. F. Bruce, said, "The most incredible feature in the Paul of popular mythology is his alleged misogyny. He treated women as persons."

A Woman's Home Becomes the
Meeting Place for the First Church in Europe

One of the women, whose name was Lydia, opened her heart and her home to Paul and his three companions, Silas, Timothy and Luke. Lydia seems to have been a woman of some means. She was a business woman who had relocated from Thyatira to Philippi to carry on her business of selling dyed garments. She must have had a sizeable estate for she had no problem accommodating these four men.

Lydia was the head of a household, which included not only immediate family, but also extended family as well as servants and their families. Luke does not tell us if she was a widow or how she had come to be the head of a household, but the fact is that when she accepted Christ and was baptized, *her household* followed her in baptism.

Lydia's home became Paul's base of operations for Philippi and the primary meeting place for the new *ekklesia* (church) in Philippi (Acts 16:15, 40). This is indicated by the fact that when Paul and Silas were later arrested and then released from jail, they immediately went to the house of Lydia where they met with the brothers and sisters and encouraged them before departing Philippi (Acts 16:40).

Think about it! The first church in Europe was begun with women and met in the home of a woman. It is incredulous to think that when the believers gathered in Lydia's house that she and the other women sat in the corner in silence while the men did all the talking. Such nonsense is based on a contorted misinterpretation of a single verse of Scripture, I Corinthians 14:34, while ignoring everything else Paul said and did in regards to women.

There is not the slightest indication that Lydia and the other women did not fully participate in the church gatherings in her home. In fact, in Paul's letter to the church at Philippi, which would have been to these same people, he speaks in respectful terms of these women *who labored with me in the gospel* (Philippians 4:3).

A Slave-Girl Delivered

The other woman we meet in Philippi is from the other end of the social spectrum as Lydia—a slave-girl who is also a fortune teller by which she brings much financial gain to her masters. Luke says this young woman *followed Paul and us*

(Acts 16:17), which may be more than a picture of her trailing along behind Paul and the rest. She, perhaps, had become a follower and identified herself with Paul and this company.

While in their midst, this young woman continually trumpeted forth a prophecy, proclaiming, *These men are servants of the Most High God who proclaim to us the way of salvation* (Act 16:17). This went on for many days until Paul, being grieved in his spirit, turned and commanded the spirit to come out of her. Even though the prophecy was true, Paul discerned that it was coming from a false spirit.

Luke describes the spirit as a *spirit of divination*. (Acts 16:16). Interestingly, the Greek word that is translated "divination" in this passage is *python*. Luke literally says that she was possessed by a "spirit of python" (Acts 16:16).

Pagan Prophecy Amongst the Greeks & Romans

Because prophecy was common among the ancient Greeks and Romans, the actions of this young woman were not strange. The noted historian, F. C. Grant, has said that the consultation of prophetic oracles was probably the most universal cult practice in the Greco-Roman world.[6]

The word *python*, which Luke used to describe the spirit that possessed this young woman, was a word commonly associated with prophecy in the ancient world. The original readers of Acts, therefore, would have made an immediate association when they read the words *spirit of python*.

The most famous ancient oracle (prophetic center) was at the city of Delphi in Greece and was known as the "Oracle at Delphi." According to legend, the Greek god, Apollo, had slain a large female serpent--a python--at that site and the spirit of the python had remained. According to the legend, it now possessed the prophets and prophetesses who functioned there, "taking possession of their organs of speech moving and compelling them to give prophetic utterances."[7]

This prophetic spirit was commonly known as the "pythian spirit" or the "spirit of python." At the height of its popularity, the oracle at Delphi maintained three prophetesses who offered advice and counsel through the pythian spirit to a continual stream of visitors including generals and government officials.

Luke uses *spirit of python* in regards to this slave girl probably because the spirit operating in her was like the one at Delphi. There is, of course, the possibility that she had actually been to Delphi and that is where she picked up this false spirit. It is important to note that what she said was true. Satan and demons have some knowledge and will reveal their "secrets" in order to impress and draw people into their destructive web. Only our God, however, is omniscient, *i.e.,* all knowing.

Victory in the Midst of Persecution

Paul discerned that the spirit was not from God and cast it out of the young woman. When the spirit went out, her fortune telling power went with it. This meant she could no longer maintain a money-making clientele for her owners.

This infuriated them and they had Paul and Silas arrested, beaten and thrown in prison (Acts 16:19-24).

In the inner dungeon with their backs caked with blood and their bodies wracked with pain, Paul and Silas, at midnight, prayed and sang praises to God. God supernaturally intervened and delivered them, resulting in the jailer and his entire household coming to faith in Jesus (Acts 25-34). No doubt many of the prisoners also became part of the Christian community in Philippi.

Although there is no hard evidence, there is reason to believe that this slave-girl's freedom was purchased by Paul, Lydia and the believers in Philippi and that she became a part of the Christian community in that city. She would have been no longer of any use to her masters. Since she was now delivered from Satan's grip, I think the believers there would have reached out to her.

The Women Who Labored with Paul

Some years later, writing from his place of imprisonment in Rome, Paul urged those in Philippi to *help these women who labored with me in the gospel* (Philippians 4:3). Gerald F. Hawthorne, in the *Word Biblical Commentary*, says that Paul, in this passage, uses a metaphor which means "to fight together side by side with," clearly indicating that Paul sees these women, not as peons under him, but as highly esteemed members of his team who have labored at his side in the cause of Christ.

To "labor" in the gospel is an all-inclusive word referring to the effort put forth in preaching, teaching, pastoring, discipling, etc. This is borne out by Jesus in Matthew 9:38

when He saw the multitudes as like *sheep without a shepherd*. He exhorted the disciples to pray the Lord of the Harvest that He would *send laborers* into His harvest.

Remember that in Greek, "shepherd" and "pastor" are both translated from the same Greek word, *poimen*. The words of Jesus in this passage thus show that the need for "shepherds" or "pastors" is fulfilled in the sending forth of "laborers." This shows that the ministry of the women who "labored" with Paul in Philippi, included that of "pastoring" or "shepherding."

Women Leaders in Philippi

Philippians is Paul's most personal and affectionate letter, and is also the only letter in which he addresses leaders. All his other letters are addressed to the congregations with no mention of their leaders. Given the nature of the founding of the church in Philippi, we can assume that women are included in the *episcopoi* (bishops) and *diakonoi* (ministers) whom Paul addresses in Philippians 1:1.

We must not complicate and impede the spread of the gospel with traditional gender and church polity issues. Paul worked with hungry hearts without regard for gender and had "church" in whatever place was appropriate and suitable at the time. We should emulate Paul and his women coworkers in Philippi and "just do it!"

Chapter 4

Paul & the Mighty Women of Macedonia

*He argued long and passionately about and for women
and their roles in his churches. He encouraged and
promoted the work of women who were his coworkers.*

Professor Ben Witherington III

J. B. Lightfoot, the noted British scholar and archaeologist, collected archaeological evidence showing that Macedonian women generally held an exceptionally honored and influential position in that culture. Inscriptions, for example, show that the mother's name is often recorded rather than the father's, and epitaphs by husbands on the tombs of their wives, contain terms markedly reverent as well as affectionate.

The well-known Cambridge scholar and Church of England bishop, the late H. C. G. Moule, said that there were two traits that stand out about the Macedonian churches of Philippi, Thessalonica and Berea. Number one, he said, was the position and influence of women, and number two was their generosity in giving both to Paul and the poor saints in Jerusalem.

This is borne out in Paul's 2nd letter to Corinth in which he commends that believers in Macedonia, saying,

Moreover, brothers and sisters, we make known to you the grace of God bestowed on the churches of Macedonia: that in a great trial of affliction the abundance of their joy and their deep poverty abounded in the riches of their generosity. For I bear witness that according to their ability, yes, and beyond their ability, they were freely willing, imploring us with much urgency that we would receive the gift . . . (II Corinthians 8:1-4).

The Egalitarian Nature of Macedonian Culture

In Thessalonica, Luke says that a great multitude of Greeks, and not a *few prominent women*, joined Paul and Silas. (Acts 17:4; NIV). The Greek word translated as "prominent" in the NIV is *proton*, and is translated as "leading" in the NKJV, "important" in the NLT, "influential" in J.B. Philips and "chief" in the ASV.

In light of this cultural equality for women in Macedonia, it is interesting that in Paul's letter to the church in Thessalonica, he pictures his ministry among them like that, not of a father, but as a nursing mother. Showing the caring, nurturing side of his personality, he writes,

Nor did we seek glory from men, either from you or from others, when we might have made demands as apostles of Christ. But we were gentle among you, just as a nursing mother cherishes her children. (I Thessalonians 1:6-7).

Paul's ministry in Macedonia began with a group of praying women in Philippi and continued with Macedonian women laboring at his side in the cause of Christ. Perhaps the openness of the women in Macedonia explains why God intervened supernaturally and directed Paul in a vision to take the gospel to that region.

Paul Supernaturally Directed to Macedonia

It was during his 2nd missionary journey that Paul received a supernatural call to take the gospel to Macedonia (Acts 16:9). Up until this time, Paul had been experiencing uncertainty as to his next field of labor. Luke indicates that he planned to take his team into the Roman province of Asia but says they were *forbidden by the Holy Spirit* do so (Acts 16:6).

Continuing on their journey to Mysia, Paul then attempted to go into Bithynia, *but the Spirit did not permit them* (Acts 16:7). From Mysia they traveled to Troas where Paul had his famous night vision of the man from Macedonia saying, *Come over to Macedonia and help us* (Acts 16:9).

Luke, the author of Acts, obviously joined Paul's team in Troas. This is indicated by the fact that when the account reaches Troas the third-person pronouns, "they" and "them," become first-person pronouns, "we" and "us." And even though only Paul saw the vision, Luke says that immediately "we" sought to go to Macedonia, *concluding that the Lord had called **us** to preach the gospel to them* (Acts 16:10).

Why did God intervene and specifically direct Paul and his companions to preach the gospel in Macedonia at this time? Could it be that the egalitarian nature of Macedonian culture provided an opening for the gospel that did not exist in the other places they tried to go? Bruce thinks so, and is certainly correct when he says, "The gospel doctrine of woman's dignity would find good soil in Macedonia."

The Prominence of Women in the Macedonian Churches

Based on the vision, Paul and his companions proceeded to Philippi, which Luke describes as *the foremost city of that part of Macedonia*. Thessalonica, the largest city of Macedonia, was further along the route being taken by Paul and his companions. It would be visited by them after their departure from Philippi.

Philippi, part of present day Bulgaria, was a major trading center since it was situated on the main highway that connected the eastern provinces of the Roman Empire with Rome. It was also a city filled with much occultic activity and idolatry. Paul and his companions arrived there probably sometime in the year 49 or 50.

As mentioned in the precious chapter, Paul began his ministry in Macedonia with a group of praying women in Philippi. In Philippi, women played a prominent role in the founding of the church and in its ongoing growth and expansion (Acts 16:13-15). This is obvious, not only in Acts, but also in Paul's letter to this church in which he appeals to certain women by name.

In Philippians 4:2, Paul appeals to two women leaders by name, Eudoia and Syntyche, and pleads with them to resolve their differences and to come together in agreement of mind and soul. The Greek of this verse indicates an

43

appeal, not only to agree mentally, but to have an agreement of heart and affection.

The attention Paul gives to this situation indicates that these women are leaders in the church in Philippi and their division has the potential to cause a division in the congregation. Paul then exhorts the entire congregation in Philippi to *help these women*, whom he says, *labored with me in the gospel* (Philippians 4:2-3).

Some think one of these women may have been Lydia since Lydia, as it is used in Acts, is an adjective, literally meaning "the Lydian." The name probably referred to her place of origin in the Roman province of Lydia, located in the region of present day western Turkey. According to this theory, those in Philippi would have referred to her, a foreigner, not just by her name, but as "the Lydian."

Be that as it may, Paul singles out these two women by name and exhorts the rest of the congregation to help them. Based on what we know of the church in Philippi, we have every reason to believe that these women are included among the *bishops and deacons* whom Paul addresses in Philippians 1:1.

The "Overseers Who Serve" in Philippi

Paul's letter to the Philippians is the only letter in which he addresses leaders in the introduction. He normally addresses his letters to the congregation without referencing a pastor, bishop, or other leader. For example, his letter to the church in Rome is addressed, *To all who are in Rome, beloved of God, called to be saints* (Romans 1:7). His first letter to Corinth is addressed, *To the Church of God which is at Corinth, to those who are sanctified in Christ Jesus, called to be saints* (I Corinthians 1:2).

In his letter to the church in Philippi, however, he addresses it first of all, *to all the saints in Christ Jesus who are in Philippi*, and then adds, *with the bishops and deacons* (Philippians 1:1).

"Bishops and deacons" in this passage is a translation of the Greek phrase *episcopoi kai diakonoi*. The NIV translates this phrase as "overseers and deacons." The NRSV offers the option of "overseers and helpers" as a translation of this phrase, and the GNT has "church leaders and helpers."

In his excellent commentary on Philippians, Professor Gerald Hawthorne, argues convincingly that *episcopoi kai diakonoi* should be translated as "overseers who serve." This is based on the fact that the Greek *kai* can serve, not only as a conjunction linking two subjects together, but also as an intensive, which in this case means that *diakonoi* serves to elaborate and intensify *episcopoi*.

Translating *episcopoi* as "overseers" is correct since the word literally means "to watch over." Not unique to the New Testament, it was used in the Greco-Roman world in reference to tutors, army scouts, watchmen on city walls and superintendents of building projects. Paul borrowed the word and used it to refer to the responsibility of Christian leaders to "watch over" the affairs of the congregation.

That *episcopas*, which is the singular form of *episcopoi*, did not originally refer to a specific church office is borne out by the fact that in Acts 20:17, 28 it is used interchangeably with "pastor" (Gk. *poimen*), and in Titus 1:5-7 it is used interchangeably with "elder" (Gk. *presbuteros*). This functional nature of the *episcopas* was confirmed by the famous church father, Augustine, who pointed out that the etymology of the word refers to responsibility and not authority. "Therefore," said Augustine, "he who loves to govern rather than do good is no bishop."[8]

The Greek word that is translated "deacons" in this passage is *diakonoi*, the plural of *diakonos*. In the New Testament era, *diakonos* was a word that referred to a lowly servant who did the bidding of his/her master. It carried no connotations of status or power, which is why the NRSV offers the option of "helper" as a translation. It was first introduced by Jesus to the Twelve in Mark 10:35-45 as the word that is to characterize His leaders.

That *diakonos* is a functional word and not a church office at this early date, is borne out by the fact that it is used by Paul on more than one occasion to describe his own ministry. In I Corinthians 3:5, for example, Paul uses *diakonoi* in regards to himself and Apollos, saying, *Who then is Paul, and who is Apollos, but ministers (Gk. diakonoi) through whom you believed.*

To summarize, *diakonos* was commonly used in the New Testament church to emphasize the "servant" character of New Testament leadership, and *episcopas* was a generic word for leaders in the New Testament church meaning to "watch over." This all gives credence to "overseers who serve" as being the best translation for *episcopoi kai diakonoi*.

Paul's Deep Concern for the Leaders in Philippi

There are probably two reasons that Paul addresses church leaders in the opening of his letter to the church in Philippi. First of all, his letter to Philippi is his most personal and affectionate letter. He obviously feels a deep connection with these men and women who suffered so much with him. This deep affection is expressed in 1:8 where he says, *For God is my witness how greatly I long for you with the affection of Jesus Christ.*

Secondly, he addresses the leaders (overseers who serve) because there is dissension and strife in their ranks, which could affect the entire congregation. He deals with this strife by emphasizing the importance of humility throughout the letter and challenging them all to follow the example of Jesus who in the Incarnation "emptied Himself" and taking the form of a bondservant, *He humbled Himself and became obedient to the point of death* (Philippians 2:5-9).

By addressing the leaders as "overseers who serve," Paul cuts to the heart of any ego and pride in their ranks and reminds them that they are servants, not rulers, of the people of God. His words also serve as a reminder to the modern reader that New Testament leadership is not about status and power over people, but service and help to people in the name of Christ.

Based on what we know of Paul's ministry in Macedonia from Acts and from his letters to Philippi and Thessalonica, we have every reason to believe that women are included in his opening greeting to the leaders in Philippi. They are among the "overseers who serve."

Chapter 5

Paul, The Egalitarian

*For as many of you as were baptized into Christ
have put on Christ. There is neither Jew nor Greek,
there is neither slave nor free, there is neither
male nor female; for you are all one in Christ Jesus.*

Paul, Galatians 3:27-28

Paul's many positive friendships and interactions with women show that he was not a male chauvinist. This is also demonstrated by his use of gender-inclusive language in his letters. Paul thought and wrote in terms of "people"—men and women—and not just in masculine terms. This is made clear in his use of three gender-related Greek words that correspond to the English words "man," "woman," and "person."

Aner is gender-specific and refers to a man (or husband depending on context) and corresponds to our English word "man." *Gunē*, which is also gender-specific, refers to a woman (or wife depending on context) and corresponds to our English word "woman." *Anthropos*, which is gender-inclusive, corresponds to our English word "person" or, in its plural form, "people."

The Skewing of Paul's Gender-Inclusive Language

Many translators have unfortunately translated the Greek word *anthropos* as "man," instead of the more accurate "people." In some passages it is understood that "man" is being used in a generic sense to refer to both men and women. This is the case with John 12:32 where the KJV has Jesus saying, *And I, if I be lifted up from the earth, will draw all men unto me.* We understand instinctively from the context that "men" is here used generically to refer to both men and women.

In other passages, however, it is not so clear that "man" should be understood generically as referring to both men and women. For example, the NKJV of II Timothy 2:2 reads, *The things you have heard from me among many witnesses, that commit to faithful **men** who shall be able to teach others also.* Because of a bias against women teaching in the church, many have assumed that this passage affirms the doctrine that only men can teach in the church.

They are, however, wrong. Paul here uses the gender-inclusive *anthropoi,* which refers to both men and women. The 2011 edition of the NIV version got it right by translating *anthropoi* as "people." It reads, *The things you have heard me say in the presence of many witnesses entrust to reliable **people** who will also be qualified to teach others.* Paul's use of *anthropoi* in this passage makes clear that he wants Timothy to raise up leaders—both men and women--in the church in Ephesus who will teach others also.

Paul also uses the gender-inclusive *anthropoi* in Ephesians 4:8 where he introduces the ministry gifts of apostle, prophet, evangelist, pastor and teacher. The passage literally reads, *Therefore He says: "When He ascended on high He led captivity captive and gave gifts to **people."** The KJV,*

NKJV and the 1984 NIV incorrectly translated *anthropoi* in this passage as "men." The 2011 NIV, NRSV and NLT have correctly translated the word as "people" demonstrating that Paul understood that these gifts would be given to both men and women.

Paul Uses Gender-Inclusive Language When Addressing Leadership in the Church

Paul, in fact, uses gender-inclusive language every time he addresses the issue of leadership in the church. For example, Paul also uses gender-inclusive language in I Timothy 3:1-5 where he discusses criteria for one serving as a bishop, or overseer. He writes,

> *This is a faithful saying: If a man (Gk. tis) desires the position of a bishop (Gk. episcopas), he desires a good work. A bishop then must be blameless, the husband of one wife . . . one who rules his own house well, having his children in submission with all reverence, for if a man (Gk. tis) does not know how to rule (manage) his own house, how will he take care of the church of God* (I Timothy 3:1-5).

Nowhere in this passage does Paul use the Greek word for man, *aner*, but instead uses the gender-inclusive personal pronoun *tis*, which means "someone" or "anyone." For example, in 3:1 it is not, *if a man* . . . as the KJV and NKJV have it, but *if anyone* (NIV) or *if someone* (NRSV).

This is also true of vs. 5 where Paul again uses *tis*, not *aner*, to confirm that oversight is not restricted to males. If Paul had wanted to exclude women from this function of oversight, he could have easily done so by using male-specific language. Instead, he uses gender-inclusive language throughout the discussion.

Many argue that Paul's statement that the *episcopas* (overseer) must be *the husband of one wife* excludes women from serving in this leadership role. Dr. Gordon Fee has rightly pointed out that just because most of the overseers in Ephesus (Timothy's location at the time of Paul's writing) may have been men, it should not be taken to mean that they all have to be men.

There is, however, a more compelling reason for this requirement—a reason that is rooted in Greco-Roman culture. In first century Greco-Roman culture it was acceptable for men to keep mistresses and carry on multiple sexual relationships, but it was not culturally acceptable for a woman to act in this manner. Women who acted in this manner would be deemed sluts and whores, but for men it was acceptable.

Interestingly, because there is not a separate word for "husband" or "wife" in Greek, this passage can read that the overseer must be "a man of one woman." Because of the culture that allowed men to be philanderers, Paul deemed it necessary to include this requirement, that relates particularly to men, to be included in this list of criteria for *tis* (anyone) who would serve as an overseer.

In I Timothy 3:5, Paul says, *If **anyone** does not know how to manage their own household* . . .. As mentioned above, Paul purposely uses the gender inclusive personal pronoun, *tis,* in this verse. As in vs. 2, it is not *if a man*, as the KJV and NKJV have it, but *if someone* (NRSV) or *if anyone* (NIV).

In addition, managing a household was not the sole province of men in Paul's world, for in his travels he had encountered women who were heads of households. In Philippi, he and his team were received by Lydia and *she and **her household** were baptized* (Acts 16:15) and her estate became the base for Paul's ministry in that city.

In I Corinthians 1:11, Paul mentions those of **Chloe's household** who had brought him unfavorable news about the Corinthians. Chloe too is a feminine name and is further proof that women managed households in the ancient world, which qualified them to serve as overseers in the church.

Inclusive Language Concerning Jesus & the Incarnation

Paul also uses *anthropos* (person) when discussing the Incarnation and the mediatorial ministry of Jesus. This shows that, for Paul, what is at stake in the Incarnation is not the maleness of Jesus but the humanity of Jesus.

> *But emptied Himself taking the form of a slave, being born in human likeness. And being found in human form, He humbled Himself and became obedient to the point of death—even death on a cross* (Philippians 2:7-8; NRSV).

For there is one God; there is also one mediator between God and humankind, Christ Jesus, Himself human. (I Timothy 1:5; NRSV).

The point is that, in the Incarnation, Jesus identified with us in our humanity and is the one Mediator for all humanity. It is obvious that Paul carefully chooses his words to make this point when speaking of the benefits and blessings of the Incarnation and of Christ's mediatorial ministry on our behalf.

A New Value System "in Christ"

Paul's conversion experience was so radical that he came into an entirely new value system "in Christ" in which the old value judgments based on race, class and gender were discarded and were no longer factors in judging a person's merit or value. He expressed this in his letter to the Galatians, perhaps his earliest letter.

For as many of you as were baptized into Christ have put on Christ. There is neither Jew nor Greek, there is neither slave nor free, there is neither male nor female; for you are all one in Christ Jesus (Galatians 3:27-28).

Paul saw that God, "in Christ," had created a new humanity that transcended all the old worldly distinctions and human classifications. In I Corinthians 5:17 he elaborates on this, saying that if anyone is "in Christ," that person is a "new creation" and that *old things have passed away; behold all things have become new.*

53

Some New Testament scholars believe Galatians 3:27-28 was part of a baptismal formula that all baptismal candidates were required to repeat. This meant that, for those earliest disciples, this new value system was a part of the basics of what it meant to be a part of this new humanity that is "in Christ."[9]

This new value system "in Christ" raised the dignity of women in the early church and it also led to the destruction of slavery in the ancient world. This occurred, not by outright opposition, but by Christians teaching and living a value system that completely undermined it and led to its collapse.

Conclusion

Evidence points strongly to the fact that Paul was egalitarian in His approach to life and ministry. This is confirmed by his deeds and by his letters in which he carefully used egalitarian language to include both men and women.

This egalitarian outlook did not come from his upbringing in Judaism or his training in Greco-Roman culture. It came, instead, from his encounter with Jesus Christ and the revelation of a new value system "in Christ" that flowed from that encounter.

Chapter 6

Did Paul Tell Women to be Silent in Church?

What then was Paul's response to the dredging up of the old idea that it was disgraceful for women to speak? Paul countered, "ἤ [Nonsense!] Did the word of God originate with you?
Loren Cunningham and David Hamilton

Many people both inside and outside the church know that Paul said something about women being silent in church. They can't tell you where the passage is found and they know nothing about the context, but they are certain that they understand what Paul meant. The truth is, however, that Paul never told women to be silent in the church.

The passage in question is I Corinthians 4:34-35 and reads,

> Let your women keep silent in the churches, for they are not permitted to speak; but they are to be submissive, as the law also says. And if they want to learn something, let them ask their own husbands at home; for it is shameful for women to speak in church.

There are several immediate and glaring problems with this passage. First of all, it is out of character with what we know of Paul from Acts and his other letters. Secondly, this passage is also out of character with what Paul has said earlier in this same letter where women are allowed to pray and prophesy if, for cultural reasons in Corinth, they wear a head covering. Thirdly, what "law" is being referred to in this passage? There is no such law in the Old Testament that demands female silence in the public assembly.

Perhaps the greatest challenge for taking this passage at face value is the fact that it is a part of a larger dialogue about Spiritual gifts and, in typical Pauline fashion, inclusive language is used throughout the discussion. In I Corinthians 14:23, for example, Paul speaks of the potential of the *whole* church coming together and *all* speaking with tongues. Then in vss. 24 & 31, he speaks of the potential for *all* to prophesy. In vs. 31 he says *all* may prophesy that *all* may learn and *all* be encouraged.

In no way does Paul imply that *all* does not mean both men and women in these verses. If he had wanted to exclude women he could have done so by using gender-specific language, but he doesn't. Verse 21 in the KJV has Paul saying, *In the Law it is written, with **men** of other tongues and other lips will I speak to this people.* "Men," however, is not in the Greek, but was added by the translators. The NRSV got it right by translating the Greek phrase as, *By **people** of strange tongues . . ..*

In a similar way, vs. 27 in the KJV has Paul saying. *If any **man** speak in an unknown tongue . . ..* Again, the KJV translators have taken a lot of freedom, for the Greek word translated "man" is *tis* and actually means "anyone." In this whole discussion about prophecy and tongues in the church, Paul is obviously careful not to exclude anyone from participating because of their gender.

We must remember too that Paul did not write in chapters and verses. These divisions were not introduced into Scripture until the fourteenth century. This means that we cannot arbitrarily lift this passage from its context, which is the discussion about Spiritual gifts where he uses gender-inclusive language, indicating his assumption that both women and men functioned in these gifts in the church gathering.

Attempts to Solve the Dilemma

Indeed, I Corinthians 14:34-35 is so out of character with the rest of this letter that it has led some good evangelical scholars to conclude that Paul did not write these verses. This is the position of Dr. Gordon Fee, a renowned New Testament exegete, who believes that an early scribe/copyist (remember they didn't have photo copiers) added these words and they found their way into the text.[10] This is certainly an option but one is left with lingering doubts by the fact that these verses are found, without exception, in every Greek manuscript.

Another solution offered by those who already have a bias against women leaders in the church, postulates that this passage bans women from judging the prophecies that come forth in the church gathering. According to this theory, women can prophesy but they cannot judge or discern the prophecies, as was commanded in 14:29. According to the proponents of this theory, women are here forbidden to judge prophecies in the congregation because this would put them in a position of authority over their husbands.

This is the position of Wayne Grudem who insists that Paul's concern in 14:34-35 is to "preserve male leadership in the teaching and governing of the church."[11] Fee, however, points out that this passage is so far removed from 14:29 that one wonders how the Corinthians themselves would have made the connection. He then takes Grudem and others to task, saying, "Nothing in the passage itself even remotely hints at such a thing."[12]

An older solution to this passage postulates a segregated church gathering with men and women seated on opposite sides of the aisles. According to this theory, Paul, in this passage, is addressing the problem of women calling to their husbands across the aisle and asking questions about what is happening in the meeting. "George, did you hear what he said?" "John, what did he mean by that"?

The problem with this theory is that it assumes a "church" situation that did not exist. There is no evidence that either Jesus or His disciples segregated the disciples according to their gender. In the Upper Room on the Day of Pentecost, men and women mingled together freely (Acts 1:14; 2:1).

This theory also assumes a traditional church setting with a "church" building with divided seating and an aisle in the middle. The fact is, however, that there is no evidence of a church building for the first two hundred years of the church's existence. During the New Testament era, Christians met primarily in homes. Their gathering itself constituted the "church," not the building in which they met. Their meetings were personal and informal and provided the context of passages such as I Corinthians 14:26

where Paul recognizes that when the Corinthians come together for "church," all are involved. *Each of you has a Psalm, has a teaching, has a tongue, has a revelation, has an interpretation . . ..*

The idea of women calling across the aisle to their husbands as the context of the passage in question, is a simplistic answer that has no basis in either Scripture or history.

The Answer is Found in One, Tiny Word

This answer to this dilemma comes to light when we recall that, in this letter, Paul addresses doctrinal questions that have been posed to him by the Corinthians in a previous letter written to him. He, no doubt, also addresses issues brought to light by members of the household of Chloe who brought him a negative report about the Corinthians and their behavior (I Corinthians 1:11). Therefore, throughout this letter Paul is responding to doctrinal questions or slogans of the Corinthians for the purpose of correcting them.

A clear example of Paul responding to the Corinthians is 7:1 where he says, *Now concerning the things of which you wrote to me: It is not good for a man to touch a woman.* There is widespread agreement among New Testament scholars that the part of the phrase, *it is not good for a man to touch a woman,* is a statement made by the Corinthians in their previous letter to Paul. He repeats it here as a means of introducing the topic and refuting their stance on the matter.

Another example is 12:1 where he says, *Now concerning Spiritual gifts,* an indication that he is now addressing questions they had posed to him about Spiritual gifts. Not only in 7:1 and 12:1, but in other sections of the letter, such as 1:12 and 3:4, Paul quotes or alludes to things the Corinthians themselves have said and then responds to their statements and slogans in order to correct them.

There is strong textual evidence that in 14:34-35, Paul is quoting what the Corinthians have said for the purpose of refuting it. This is indicated by Paul's use of a tiny Greek word at the beginning of vs. 36, and immediately following the statement about women being silent. It is the word η, which is sometimes used in Greek as an "expletive of disassociation," such as the English, "Nonsense!" or "Rubbish!" or "Certainly not!"[13]

Although the word can have various uses, depending on context, this use was not uncommon in the New Testament era. It is, in fact, used several times in this manner by Paul in this letter. Unfortunately, in most English Bibles, the η has been either left untranslated or translated by a simple "or," which serves to diminish the forceful manner in which Paul is using it.

One example is 6:1 is where he mentions the propensity of the Corinthians to take one another to pagan courts rather than submitting their contentions to fellow believers. He responds with η (Nonsense!) and then says, *Do you not know that the saints will judge the world?* Another example is 9:8 where Paul confronts their suggestion that he is speaking on his own authority with η (Nonsense!) and then says, *Does not the law say the same also?*

In his book, *Beyond Sex Roles*, Dr. Gilbert Bilezikian lays out the numerous instances in I Corinthians of η being used as a rebuttal by Paul and then says,

> In most cases cited above, the pattern is similar. A proposition is presented in the form of a rhetorical question or a declarative statement containing an element of incongruity. It is followed by the particle η which is used to introduce the counterstatement in the form of a question. As indicated above, the consistent use of η in each of these ten instances could be accurately rendered by substituting an indignant "nonsense."[14]

This use of η to refute a previous statement is confirmed by the massive *Greek-English Lexicon* by Liddell and Scott, which gives a definition of η as "an exclamation expressing disapproval."

This means that in I Corinthians 14:34-35 Paul is quoting what the Corinthians have said about women being silent and then replies with "an exclamation expressing disapproval." He says, "η," meaning "Nonsense!"

Paul then uses η a second time in vs. 36. After the first η, in which he rebuts their notion of women being silent, he asks the Corinthians, *Did the word of God originate with you,* and follows that question with anther η, or "Certainly not!"

Conclusion

This interpretation of I Corinthians 14:34-35 makes the best sense of the data and harmonizes this verse with the rest of the letter and with everything we know about Paul and how he treated women. It fits the Paul we know from Acts and his letters who treated women with respect, acknowledged their gifts, and recognized them as co-laborers with him in the Gospel.

Chapter 7

Paul on Sex &
Marriage in Corinth

He delighted in the company of his fellows, both men and women.
The most incredible feature in the Paul of popular mythology
is his alleged misogyny. He treated women as persons.

F. F. Bruce, New Testament Scholar

Corinth was "sin city" of the ancient world. Known throughout the Empire for the immoral decadence of its inhabitants, Corinth had such a reputation in this regard that a word was coined, *korinthiazo,* for anyone who was blatantly and sexually immoral. It meant "to act like a Corinthian."

Corinth was a large and flourishing commercial center, perhaps the third largest city of the Roman Empire, after Rome and Alexandria. According to the ancient historian, Strabo, Old Corinth (before the Romans took the city in 146 B.C.) was home of the famous temple of the goddess Aphrodite, which was serviced by one thousand prostitute-priestesses who also plied their trade throughout the city.

This immoral character of the city is reflected in the Christian community, for in his letters to the church in Corinth, Paul addresses sexual sins, including incest, as well as cliques, drunkenness, and abuse of spiritual gifts.

63

Paul's Weak & Broken Condition Upon Arriving in Corinth

Paul arrived in Corinth around A. D. 50 in a broken and weakened condition, both physically and emotionally (I Corinthians 2:1-5). He describes his condition at the time in terms of his weaknesses, not his strengths. Writing after the fact, he reminds the Corinthians how, *I was with you in weakness, in fear and in much trembling* (I Corinthians 2:3).

"Weakness" in this verse is from the Greek word *asthenia* and means "to be powerless and without strength." "Fear" is from the Greek word *phobo* (from which we get "phobia") and, according to *Thayer's Greek-English Lexicon*, means "to be struck with terror and fear." "Much trembling" is from the Greek work *tromo* (from which we get "trauma" and "traumatized") and according to *Thayer's Greek English Lexicon*, means "to shake and tremble with fear and dread."

In other words, Paul does not arrive as the great apostle ready to take the city for God. His description of himself sounds as if he is almost an emotional basket case. Perhaps this is where he learned the principle that he later expresses in II Corinthians 12:9-10 that God's strength is made perfect, or maximized, in weakness and, *when I am weak, then I am strong.*

Paul did not wallow in his weakness or turn inward to self, but looked away to Jesus and saw a demonstration of God's Spirit and power in Corinth. God's power was maximized in Paul's weakness and a lively—if sometimes rowdy—church was established in that decadent, pagan city.

He Makes Lifelong Friends in Corinth

In Corinth Paul met a Jewish couple, Priscilla and Aquilla, who would become lifelong friends and coworkers. While in Corinth he stayed in their home and worked with them in their tent making business. With their home and business as his base, he dialogued in the synagogue each Sabbath and persuaded many that Jesus was the promised Messiah (Acts 18:1-4).

When opposition arose in Corinth (as it had in other cities), the Lord spoke a word of encouragement to Paul in a vision, saying, *Do not be afraid, but speak, and do not be silent; for I am with you, and no one will attack you to hurt you for I have many people in this city* (Acts 18:9-10).

After at least 18 months in Corinth, Paul departed taking Priscilla and Aquilla with him. They stopped in Ephesus where Aquilla and Priscilla remained while Paul continued his journey toward Jerusalem. He would follow up his time in Corinth with later visits and at least three (maybe four) letters to the believers in that city.

Sexual Extremes in Corinth

In I Corinthians 7:1-12 Paul presents his most extensive teaching on marriage and it is the only one in which he uses the word "authority." This teaching on marriage is his response to a question about sex and marriage they had posed in a letter to Paul.

That he is responding to a question from them is obvious from the fact that he opens the discussion in I Corinthians

7:1 by saying, *Now concerning the things of which you wrote to me: It not good for a man to touch (have sexual relations with) a woman.*

As mentioned in the previous chapter, many New Testament scholars believe that when Paul says, *It is not good for a man to touch (have sexual relations with) a woman,* that he is repeating what the Corinthians have said in their letter to him. C. K. Barrett, for example, notes the difficulty in interpretation that is removed by this perspective,[15] and Gordon Fee readily assumes that Paul is quoting the Corinthians in order to introduce his response.[16]

This statement from the Corinthians indicates that, along with sexual laxity in their midst, there has emerged a super-spiritual group on the other end of spectrum that would refrain from sex completely, even in marriage. Such extremes have emerged throughout history with certain groups teaching that sex was the original sin and to be a part of the spiritual elite one must refrain from all sex, even in marriage.

This sort of thinking is behind the Catholic Church's requirement that her priests be celibate. It seems to be the case in Corinth for in 7:28 Paul finds it necessary to tell the unmarried that if they marry, they have not sinned. That such teaching is making the rounds in Corinth is indicated by the fact that Paul also finds it necessary to exhort the married couples to not deprive one another of sex, except during temporary times set apart for prayer and fasting.

66

Paul's Most Extensive Teaching on Marriage

In his response to their inquiry about marriage, Paul lays out a marriage relationship in which there is mutuality with shared and equal authority (7:1-14). It is his most extensive teaching on marriage and the only one in which he uses the word "authority" (Gk. *exousia*). In every case he gives equal authority to the wife as he does to the husband. Commenting on this, Fee says,

> In a way quite unlike anything else in all his letters, the argument alternates between men and women (12 times in all). And in every case there is complete mutuality between the sexes.[17]

Examples of this are as follows.

1. Let each man have his own wife and let each woman have her own husband (vs. 2).

2. Let the husband render to his wife the affection due her and likewise also the wife to her husband (vs. 3).

3. The wife does not have authority over her own body, but the husband does. And likewise the husband does not have authority over his own body, but the wife does (vs. 4)

4. Do not deprive one another except with consent (vs. 5).

5. A wife is not to depart from her husband. And a husband is not to divorce his wife (vs. 10).

6. For the unbelieving husband is sanctified by the wife, and the unbelieving wife is sanctified by the

husband; otherwise your children would be unclean, but now they are holy (vs. 14).

The Husband is Blessed Because of the Wife

In this discussion, Paul completely dispels the modern notion that God works through a male hierarchy and that a woman must be under the spiritual authority of a male. He shows, instead, that an unbelieving husband and the entire household will be blessed as the result of the faith of a believing wife and mother. He writes,

> *And if a woman who has a husband who does not believe, if he is willing to live with her, let her not divorce him. For the unbelieving husband is sanctified by the wife, and the unbelieving wife is sanctified by the husband; otherwise your children would be unclean, but now they are holy (I Corinthians 7:13-14).*

The word "willing" in the above verse is translated from the Greek word *suneudokei*, which means "to approve together" or "to consent together." In other words, if an unbelieving husband, with the wife's approval and consent, is willing to live with her, he will be blessed because of her faith. In fact, God's blessing will come to the entire home because of her faith.

In saying that the unbelieving spouse will be "sanctified," Paul is not saying that they will be saved. He is merely saying that by being in the home with a believing wife or husband, the unbelieving spouse will partake of the blessing that comes through the believing spouse.

Paul is clear, however, that there must be mutual consent. So long as an unbelieving husband does not resist or come against his believing wife, he will be blessed because of her faith.

Concluding Thought

It is interesting that Paul's most extensive teaching on marriage is hardly mentioned in evangelical seminars, books, or manuals on marriage. Could it be because it does not easily fit into the hierarchical model of marriage to which so many have religiously committed themselves?

Chapter 8

Paul Confronts Magic & Marriage in Ephesus

Magicians and astrologers swarmed in her streets and there was a brisk trade in the charms, incantations, books of divination, rules for interpreting dreams, and the like.
Charles Ellicott

Ephesus was the largest city of the Roman province of Asia and known in the ancient world for two things: (1) worship of the mother goddess, Artemis, who's massive and ornate temple was in Ephesus; and (2) the practice of magic and sorcery.

Worship of Artemis

The imposing temple dedicated to Artemis (called Diana by the Romans) was 425 feet long, 220 feet wide and was adorned with 127 ornate columns that were 60 feet in height. The temple took 220 years to build and was considered one of the Seven Wonders of the ancient world. Visitors and religious pilgrims came from all over the ancient world to view this massive, ornate structure and to worship at its shrine.

Modern archaeology has shown that Ephesus was likely founded by a small group of Artemis devotees who built a small shrine in her honor. As more devotees to the mother goddess were attracted to the area, it developed into a major city in the ancient world. Over time the residents were able to fund the building of the magnificent temple in honor of Artemis.

The point is that the city's very existence was rooted in the worship of Artemis. Luke reveals that the city's economy was, to a great degree, based on the steady stream of religious pilgrims who came from all over the Greco-Roman world to view the magnificent temple and worship at its shrine.

Magic & the Occult

Ephesus was also known as a center of sorcery and magic. Charles Ellicott, in his *Commentary* on Acts 19:19, says,

> Magicians and astrologers swarmed in her streets and there was a brisk trade in the charms, incantations, books of divination, rules for interpreting dreams, and the like.

The proliferation of magical incantations and formulas in Ephesus were collected into a book known as the "Ephesian letters" and spread throughout the Greco-Roman world. Albert Barnes, in his *Notes* on this passage, says,

> The Ephesian letters, by which incantations and charms were supposed to be produced, were much celebrated. They seem to have consisted of certain combinations of letters or words, which, by being pronounced with certain intonations of voice, were

believed to be effectual in expelling diseases, or evil spirits; or which, by being written on parchment and worn, were supposed to operate as amulets, or charms, to guard from evil spirits or from danger.

Paul's Mode of Operation in Confronting the Evil in Ephesus

Paul did not react to the Ephesian culture and go on a tirade against Artemis. He went to Ephesus in A.D. 52 with complete confidence in the power of the name of Jesus and the power of the message he preached.

As was his custom, Paul began his ministry in Ephesus in the Jewish synagogue. When, after three months, opposition arose from within the synagogue, Paul removed himself and the disciples to a public lecture hall known as the "School of Tyrannus" (Acts 19:9-10).

Luke tells us that Paul spent the next two years *reasoning daily* in this lecture hall. The word "reasoning" is translated from the Greek word *dialegomenous*, from which we get the word "dialogue." The NIV says that he held "daily discussions."

The point Luke makes by using the word *dialegomenous* is that Paul was giving people the opportunity to ask questions and challenge what he was teaching. He was not just preaching sermons and then departing. Paul made room for dialogue and discussion because he wanted to make sure that the Ephesian populace understood the truth, for only the truth would set them free, as Jesus had said in John 8:31-32.

With Ephesus being both a commercial and religious center, many of the visitors obviously stopped in to hear Paul's daily discussions. This is confirmed by Luke statement that during the next two years, *all who dwelt in Asia heard the word of the Lord Jesus, both Jews and Greeks* (Acts 19:10).

Interestingly, there is no mention of any of the popular modes of spiritual warfare so popular in charismatic circles today. For example, Paul did not dress in military clothing and shout and scream commands at a spirit of Artemis. He knew that the people of Ephesus were held in bondage by lies and deceptions. He therefore gave priority to communicating truth, knowing that the truth would set the inhabitants free of the various bondages in which they were ensnared.

This is Paul's point in II Corinthians 10:3-5 where he speaks of the *weapons of our warfare*. In vs. 5 he speaks of using these weapons to cast down, or topple, *arguments*, which the KJV calls *imaginations. Casting down arguments and every high thing that exalts itself against the knowledge of God.*

The word "arguments" (or "imaginations") in this passage is translated from the Greek word *logismous*, which is from *logos* and is often translated as "word." But as *Thayer's Greek-English Lexicon* points out, *logos* differs from *rhema* in the since that it is a word that "embodies a concept or idea," i.e., a belief system.

Paul knew that the people of Ephesus were held in bondage by a false *logismous*, or belief system. Only the truth would set them free It would be a waste of time to scream and shout at a spirit of Diana. Only the truth of God's word would topple the demonic forces that held the people in their grasp by the lies and false belief systems that were rampant throughout the city.

In examining Paul's ministry in Ephesus, it is obvious that there are two spiritual weapons that he used with great effectiveness: (1) the Name of Jesus, and (2) the Word of God.

The Power of the Name

We know that Paul taught and used the authority of the name of Jesus for certain Jewish exorcists who heard him decided to follow his example and use the name of Jesus to try and exorcise a demon. They thought, however, that they could use the name of Jesus as an incantation or magical formula. They spoke to the demons, saying, *We exorcise you by the Jesus whom Paul preaches* (Acts 19:13-16).

The demon was not impressed and answered back, *Jesus I know and Paul I know; but who are you* (Acts 19:15)? The man in whom the demon dwelt then leaped upon the exorcists, overpowered them, and injured them. Luke says, *So they fled out of that house naked and wounded* (Acts 19:16).

Their experience shows the fallacy of trying to function with a "second-hand faith." The statement of the exorcists, *in the name of Jesus whom Paul preaches*, revealed that they had no personal knowledge of Jesus or relationship with Him.

This passage also shows the fallacy of seeking to minister deliverance and healing from a superstitious, formulaic approach. No doubt influenced by the superstitious culture of Ephesus, these individuals thought they could use the names of Jesus and Paul as magical incantations or charms.

There is power in the name of Jesus, but it comes through relationship, not by just repeating the words in a mechanical manner. As believers living in relationship with Jesus, we know that we have been given authority through His name. When we command demons to depart, they will depart whether we actually say the word "Jesus" or not, because the demons know that we know that we are speaking and acting in His name.

These Jewish exorcists failed, not because they used the wrong words or formula, but because they did not have a relationship with Jesus; and the demon knew it by how they phrased their command.

When word spread of what had happened to these individuals and what the demon had said to them, Luke says, *Fear fell on them all, and the name of the Lord Jesus was magnified* (Acts 19:17). There was then a great mass movement to Christianity, with Luke saying,

> And many who had believed came confessing and telling their deeds. Also many of those who had magic brought their books together and burned them in the sight of all. And they counted up the value of them, and it totaled fifty thousand pieces of silver (Acts 1:18-19)

There is power in the name of Jesus!

The Power of the Message

Luke's account of Paul's ministry in Ephesus shows that he relied on the power that is inherent in the gospel message itself. This should not be surprising for in Romans 1:16 Paul wrote, *For I am not ashamed of the gospel of Christ, for it is the power of God to salvation for everyone who believes, for the Jew first and also for the Greek.*

Paul's confidence in the power of the message is highlighted by the fact that in the pagan city of Ephesus he focused on "dialoguing" with the populace to make sure they understood the message he was presenting to them. He did not try and "spruce up" the message and make it more attractive to the Ephesian culture for that, he knew, could lead to a loss of the substance and power that is in the message.

This is the point of I Corinthians 1:17 where Paul reminds the Corinthians that he did not use *lofty words and brilliant ideas to tell you God's message* (I Corinthians 2:1; NLT). In 1:17 he declares that God called him to preach the gospel, *not with words of human wisdom, **lest the cross of Christ be emptied of its power*** (NIV).

Paul seems to be warning that if we go too far in trying to make the gospel cool, hip and acceptable to contemporary culture, we run the risk of preaching a message that is emptied of its power. The power is in the message.

In 2000 Sue and I participated in a week-long doctoral seminar on the subject of world missions. It was a grueling week with eight-hour days sitting through lectures and discussions about strategies and methodologies for taking the gospel message to all the world.

On Thursday afternoon, somebody suggested that we pray. Sue laid her head on the table at which she was sitting, thankful for the opportunity to close her eyes and rest while everyone prayed. Suddenly, however, the Spirit of God hit her like a bolt of lightning and she began to weep and intercede in the Spirit.

Out of that intense time of intercession, God spoke this very powerful word to us.

> You have been talking all week about methods and strategies for taking the gospel message to the world, but I am concerned about the message you are taking. I want to purge the message. I want it to be My message that you take to the world.

Luke's account shows that Paul was focused on presenting the gospel message in Ephesus, rather than reacting to everything that was wrong in the Ephesian culture. This was borne out when a riot broke out, incited by certain craftsmen who were concerned that their business was going to be affected because of all the people Paul was turning from Artemis to Christ. They also expressed concern that her great temple would be despised and that the goddess herself would be diminished in honor.

A huge crowd gathered in the outdoor stadium, that would accommodate twenty-thousand people, and for two hours shouted in unison, "Great is Artemis of the Ephesians." When, however, the town clerk had quieted the mob, he pointed out that there was no evidence that Paul had blasphemed their goddess during the three years he had been there preaching. He then dismissed the gathering.

If that were today, can you imagine all the books, sermons, DVDs and CDs that would have been produced on how to pull down and overcome the Artemis spirit? Yet, there was no evidence that Paul had preached a sermon against her during the three years he had been there.

He had, instead, been teaching and preaching the gospel of Jesus Christ. He obviously was aware of the words of Jesus in John 8:32, *And you shall know the truth and the truth shall make you free.*

This is not to say that we should never confront evil. We must and there is a time and place for that. However, we must guard against becoming preoccupied with all that is not right and spending all our time reacting to those things instead of preaching the only message that has the power to change hearts and make things right.

People were forsaking Artemis and turning to Jesus because of Paul's proactive Christ-centered message that offered a new value system that did not recognize traditional, social classifications based on race, gender and class. Luke explained the change that was coming over Ephesus by saying, *So the word of the Lord grew mightily and prevailed* (Acts 19:20).

Paul's Advice to the Ephesians about Marriage

In his letter to the Ephesians, Paul gives instructions on marriage that have been used, more than any other passage, to formulate a modern "order" of marriage in which authority is given exclusively to the man. Paul's instructions, however, must be understood in the cultural context of the sort of marriage practiced by the Ephesians.

Marriage Without Hand

The Ephesians practiced a form of marriage known as "Marriage Without Hand," meaning marriage without commitment. This form of marriage was instituted by Augustus Caesar before the time of Christ in an attempt to deal with widespread wife abuse in the Roman Empire.

In "Marriage Without Hand" the wife remained under the authority of her father or oldest male in her biological family, rather than under the authority of her husband. If a father believed his daughter was being abused, he had the legal right to end the marriage and remove her from her husband's home. Her dowry (inheritance) also remained with her biological family so long as she returned home at least once per year for an overnight stay in the home of her father.

This form of marriage, however, created more problems than it solved for it did not deal with the core issue of female inequality and subordination. It actually resulted in a lack of commitment of the husband toward the wife since he knew he could lose her at any time. It resulted in the wife tending to maintain closer ties with her birth family than with her husband since she was legally tied to them rather than to her husband. Also, a father-in-law could put great pressure on a son-in-law to do his bidding by threatening to remove his daughter from him.

This form of marriage destroyed intimacy in the marriage relationship and hindered the formation of a new family unit. It often left the wife feeling like a stranger in her husband's home and the husband feeling that the wife was married to her biological family rather than to him, which was legally the case. It weakened the family structure and thereby the social fabric of the empire.

Realizing that this approach to marriage created more problems than it solved, the first legal steps to remove it as a law were made around A.D. 50 just a couple of years before Paul arrived in Ephesus. Nonetheless, because of custom and tradition, it was the most common form of marriage practiced by the Ephesians.

The Meaning of "Submit" in Ephesians

Paul's admonitions about marriage in Ephesians 5:21-33 must, therefore, be interpreted in light of the kind of marriage the Ephesians practiced, *i.e.*, Marriage Without Hand. When this is done, it then becomes obvious that he is issuing a call for mutual commitment and intimacy in the marriage relationship, and he is obviously very careful in his choice of words in making this point.

For example, in vss. 21-22 of this passage, Paul calls on the wife to *hupotasso* her husband, and *hupotasso* is the word that is translated as "submit" in our English Bibles. However, the word "submit" has been added by the translators to vs. 22. The verse actually has no verb, which means it is not a complete sentence, and literally reads, *wives to your own husbands.*

Paul has carefully crafted his exhortation so that the verb for vs. 22 is found in vs. 21 where all believers are told to *hupotasso* one another, including husbands to wives. The verb for vs. 22 is thus found in vs. 21 making it impossible to use this passage to set up a hierarchical order of marriage where there is a one-way submission of the wife to the husband.

This is why *Bauer's Greek-English Lexicon* rejects the traditional meaning of "to come under" for *hupotasso* in this passage. Bauer rightly points out that such a definition is impossible since the "submission" wives are to show husbands in vs. 22 is the same "submission" all believers are to show one another in vs. 21. Bauer, therefore, opts for a definition of "a voluntary yielding in love," which would apply to all believers.

Bauer has a point and is right to dispense with the traditional definition of "to come under" for this verse, which is the only definition given by Strong's Concordance. Strong's is a good resource for most words, but because of its brevity and age, it does not reflect the findings of modern research and archaeological discoveries that have shone much light on critical words in this passage such as *hupotasso.*

In light of the kind of marriage practiced by the Ephesians, the best definition of *hupotasso* in this passage is "to join together" or "to identify with." This meaning was not uncommon in the ancient world for both Josephus, a contemporary of Paul, and Ignatius of Antioch, a church leader in the early second century, used *hupotasso* in referring to the joining together of two documents.[18]

The massive *Greek-English Lexicon* by Liddell and Scott confirms this meaning of being "joined together" or "identified with" for this passage. It offers several meanings for *hupotasso*, each depending on the situation and context of its use. One of the meanings listed is "to be associated with."

Used like this, *hupatasso* gives the sense of the wife being "joined to" or "identified with" her husband, which did not happen in Marriage Without Hand. This is why Dr. Susan Hyatt, after extensive examination of this passage, has concluded that Paul is here calling on the wife to be identified with her husband rather than with her birth family[19]. This is confirmed by the well-known classical Greek scholar, the late Dr. Catherine Kroeger, who says, "*hupatasso* may imply "to join one thing to another," "to relate one thing to another in a meaningful fashion," "to identify one thing with another."[20]

What we have here, in Ephesians 5:21-22, is Paul calling on the woman to leave her biological family and be "identified with" her husband. In the same way that Genesis 2:24 had commanded the man to leave his father and mother and be joined to his wife, Paul now calls on the wife to leave her birth family and be identified with her husband in Christian marriage.

The Call for Husbands to Love their Wives

That Paul is issuing a call for commitment and intimacy in marriage is confirmed by his exhortation for husbands to *love your wives, just as Christ also loved the Church and gave Himself for her.* (Ephesians 5:25). With this exhortation he calls on the Ephesian husbands to dispense with any tenuousness or reluctance rooted in their traditional form of marriage, and give themselves completely to their wives.

That Paul uses the word *agape* in his exhortation to husbands was revolutionary. *Agape* is a word that refers to sacrificial love that is willing to give up one's own self-interests for the good of another. *Agape* has been called "the God-kind of love" because it is the word that is used when Scripture speaks of God's love for humanity or Christ's love for God.

Greek writers had called on husbands to rule their wives with benevolence but none had ever dared call on husbands to *agape* their wives. Commenting on this exhortation to husbands, Dr. Berkeley and Alvera Mickelsen write,

> The concept of sacrificial self-giving so that a spouse can achieve full potential has been the role that society has traditionally given to the wife. Here Paul gives it to the husband. Of course, giving oneself sacrificially for the other is an excellent example of the submission wives and husbands are to have toward one another.[21]

During the first year of our marriage Sue and I had a disagreement and neither of us was willing to yield any

83

ground. Being young and naïve and having a traditional view of marriage, I went to prayer asking God to help her understand that she must submit to my God-ordained leadership.

As I prayed in this manner, Paul's exhortation for husbands to love their wives *as Christ loved the Church* suddenly stood before me with the words **and gave Himself for her** highlighted in bold letters (Ephesians 5:25). I then heard the Holy Spirit say, "The problem is that you are not willing to let go of yourself."

When I heard this message from the Lord I knew that my "I" or *ego* was standing in the way of resolution and peace. As I obeyed the Lord and "let go of myself" in that situation, it proved to be a life-changing experience. It was my first experience of learning what Paul really meant when he called on husbands to love (*agape*) their wives.

The Meaning of "Head" in the Marriage Relationship

In Ephesians 5:23 Paul says that the husband is the "head" of the wife. The word "head" is a translation of the Greek word *kephale*, which in most places refers to the literal head on one's shoulders. Paul uses *kepahle* here in a figurative way to refer to the husband as the source or origin of the wife. That this is the meaning in Paul's usage here was demonstrated in a landmark study by Dr. Berkeley and Alvera Michelsen entitled "The Head of the Epistles," published in the Feb. 20, 1981 edition of *Christianity Today*.

By referring the husband as the source of the wife, Paul is here referring to the Genesis account of creation where, instead of creating a separate creature from the ground to make the woman, God took a side from the person He had already created from the dust, and built the side into the woman. The popular Jewish commentary known as *The Chumash*, says,

> Unlike man's, the woman's body was not taken from the earth. God built one side of the man into woman—so that the single human being became two, thereby demonstrating irrefutably the equality of man and woman."[22]

This was important for ancient teaching said that woman had been made from a different and inferior source than man, which became the basis for male superiority and female subservience. It also became the basis for homosexuality, for as Plato declared, "the truly noble soul is masculine and will therefore seek out another male as the object of its love," because they are alike and of the same substance.

Paul's use of *kephale* carried connotations of mutuality between the man and the woman and undermined the ancient argument for homosexuality. It also contributed to Paul's call for commitment and intimacy in the marriage relationship by highlighting the common origin of the sexes.

Conclusion

When seen against the background of the kind of marriage practiced by the Ephesians, it is obvious that Paul is calling for mutual commitment and intimacy between one man and one woman in the marriage relationship, and is not setting up a legal order of marriage.

Some will argue, "but what do you do when you and your spouse cannot agree on an issue?" In forty plus years of marriage we have never come to that place. Yes, we have had many disagreements, but when we have gone to our knees and sought the mind of the Lord, He has been faithful to speak to one or the other to defer in that particular situation.

In other words, we have found that death to self is an important key for a successful marriage. As long as ego and selfish pride have any place in a marriage there will not be peace and harmony. A godly and successful marriage will require two deaths and a resurrection.

Chapter 9

Paul & the Teachers of False Doctrine in Ephesus

Translation and interpretation are crucial. The proper interpretation can release women to serve wherever God may call them, or it can consign one half of the church to leave its world-wide ministry to the other half.

Richard and Catherine Kroeger

I Timothy 2:11-12 has been used more than any other passage of Scripture to restrict the role of women in the church. For many it has become the canon within the canon concerning women and they read every other passage about women through the lens of this one passage. It reads,

> Let a woman learn in silence with all submission. And I do not permit a woman to teach or to have authority over a man, but to be in silence.

The key to understanding this passage, and any passage of Scripture, is context. Understanding both the literary context and the historical context, or "life-setting," is essential for accurately interpreting this verse or any verse of Scripture.

The Importance of Context

The importance of "context" for understanding any kind of literature was highlighted to me in a personal and humorous experience. As a teenager, there was a country song in which I understood one line to say, "I had me a girl away cross Georgia." Growing up in Texas and knowing little of the geography and terrain of Georgia, I interpreted the songwriter to be saying, "I had me a girl away cross on the other side of Georgia."

After I was grown and in the ministry, I was driving across Georgia when I had a *eureka* moment about that line of the song. It happened when I came to a town named "Waycross." Until then I had no idea there was a town called Waycross, Georgia. I suddenly realized that the songwriter (who was obviously from Georgia) was not saying that he had a girl away cross on the other side of Georgia, but in the town of Waycross, Georgia.

Being in Georgia and becoming acquainted with the towns and geographical terrain of the state, gave me accurate understanding of what the writer was actually saying in that line of his song.

Now, we are far more removed from the terrain and setting of the Biblical writers than I was from the writer of that song. Because we know so little about the cultural terrain and life setting of the Biblical writers, it is so easy for words, phrases and concepts to be misunderstood and misinterpreted.

Understanding the context of Scripture, therefore, can make all the difference in the world. Understanding the cultural terrain and life setting of Paul and the person or congregation to whom he is writing, can give clarity to passages that seem obscure and hard to understand. This is especially true of the passage before us.

The Context of I Timothy

One important key to interpreting the above passage is the fact that Paul's concern in this letter is not church order or women in leadership, but the teaching of false doctrine by both men and women. This is born out in 1:3 where Paul says to Timothy, *As I urged you when I went into Macedonia-- remain in Ephesus that you may charge some that they teach no other doctrine.*

The phrase "no other doctrine" in this verse is a translation of the one Greek word, *heterodidaskelein*. This word literally means "different doctrine." It comes from two Greek words; *heteros* meaning "other" or "different," and *didaskelein* meaning "teaching" or "doctrine." The NIV translates this word as "false doctrine," the NASB as "strange doctrines," and the NRSV as "different doctrine."

This verse clearly shows that Timothy's purpose for being in Ephesus is to confront false teaching. It is also clear that Paul's purpose in writing this letter to Timothy is to encourage and instruct him in his unpleasant task. This understanding provides the setting for accurately interpreting what Paul is saying in this letter.

The traditional view that Paul wrote 1 Timothy to provide a church manual to guide the church organizationally is simply not true. Dr. Gordon Fee, Professor Emeritus of New Testament at Regent College, tells of the first time he taught 1 Timothy from the standpoint of it being, not a manual of church order, but a personal letter addressing specific issues related to Timothy being in Ephesus. He says,

> The results astonished us. And after a few more times through the PE (Pastoral Epistles) with other classes, I became fully convinced of the correctness of this point of view. It is exactly how one makes the best sense of all the earlier letters of Paul, and for me and several generations of seminarians, it has become the key for understanding the PE as well."[23]

That 1 Timothy is a personal letter written to an individual for the purpose of addressing the specific issue of false doctrine in Ephesus provides a context for helping us arrive at an accurate translation of 1 Timothy 2:11-12

The Historical Setting of I Timothy

According to 2nd century writers, Paul was released from his first Roman imprisonment of Acts 28 during which he had written the "Prison Epistles," which included Ephesians, Philippians, Colossians, and Philemon. After his release, he enjoyed a time of freedom before he was arrested a second time and imprisoned in Rome. During his second Roman imprisonment he wrote II Timothy, which was his final letter before his death at the hands of a Roman executioner.

It was during this time of freedom, between his first and second Roman imprisonments, that Paul and Timothy returned to Ephesus for a time of ministry. On this return visit they found the church in Ephesus, which consisted of many house churches (Acts 20:20), being corrupted by false teaching.

When the time came for them to depart, Paul *urged* Timothy to remain and continue dealing with the erring teachers/leaders (1:3). The fact that Paul *urged* him to stay indicates that Timothy was reluctant to do so.

There are indications that Timothy's personality was inclined to avoid confrontation. The fact that he is experiencing stomach problems and other *infirmities* (5:23) may well be related to the stress he is experiencing in confronting the erring leaders in Ephesus.

Paul convinced Timothy to remain and departed for Macedonia. Somewhere along the way, probably from Macedonia, he wrote this letter to encourage his *son in the faith* (1:2) and to instruct him in his unpleasant task of confronting the false teachers and teaching in Ephesus.

Exegeting the Passage

The best interpretation of I Timothy 2:11-12 is that Paul is addressing a specific situation in Ephesus that is having a particular effect on the women. He may also be addressing a particular woman (she may be representative of a company of women) who is propagating the "other doctrine" about which he is so concerned.

That this is the case may be indicated by the fact that prior to 2:11 in verses 9-10, Paul addresses the "women" in Ephesus; but when he comes to the prohibition of verse 11 he switches to the singular and speaks of "a woman" in Ephesus.

This interpretation is also borne out by the phrase in 2:12, *I do not permit*, which, in the Greek, is in the present, ongoing sense and literally reads, "I am not permitting." This seems to point to a restriction specific to the current situation in Ephesus, with the meaning, "I am not permitting at this time."[24]

Paul is concerned about this woman's teaching, not because she is a woman but because of what she is teaching. The situation may change if she recognizes the error of her ways. In such case, she will be allowed to teach again.

The problem of false teaching in Ephesus is being propagated by both women and men, and Paul seems to deal more harshly with the men. He mentions two of the men by name, Hymenaeus and Alexander, whom he describes as having rejected faith and a good conscience and says, *as concerning the faith have suffered shipwreck* (I Timothy 1:19:20).

This is serious for what has been shipwrecked is not their ability to believe God, but the gospel itself, which they have perverted. This is made clear by the definite article being placed before the word "faith." In other words, it is "the faith" — the gospel itself--that they have shipwrecked.

As far as Paul is concerned, their shipwreck of "the faith" amounts to blasphemy. He, therefore, deals with them severely, informing Timothy, *whom I have delivered unto Satan that they may learn not to blaspheme* (1:19-20). Knowing, perhaps, that the woman has not had the opportunity to learn, Paul says, *Let the woman learn in silence with all submission* (I Timothy 2:11).

That Paul would have women learn is revolutionary since both Jewish and Greco-Roman culture was very biased against women being educated. The New Testament scholar, Dr. Craig Keener, comments on this verse, saying,

> The way for any novice to learn was submissively and quietly. Given the bias against instructing women in the law, it is Paul's advocacy of their learning the law, not that they started as novices and so had to learn quietly, that was radical and countercultural.[25]

The Greek word for "silence" in these verses is *hesuchia* and it is the same word used in 2:2 where it is said to be God's will for all His people. *Hesuchia* refers to a life without upset and turmoil. Learning in *hesuchia, i.e.,* in calmness and quietness, was the Greek-Socratic method for all students to learn. Paul wants this woman (and all women) to be able to learn in this sort of quiet and peaceful environment, without upset and turmoil. Keener is right! Paul's admonition to allow women to learn was revolutionary in the ancient world!

Conclusion

I Timothy was not written to lay out a church order and legislate who can and cannot teach in the church. Paul wrote I Timothy to encourage his son in the faith who is carrying out the difficult task of confronting the false teachers and the doctrines they are propagating in Ephesus.

It is not women *per se* that Paul wants Timothy to silence in Ephesus; it is false teachers, both men and women, that he wants to silence. This will be further borne out by Paul's use of strange Greek word in 2:12.

Chapter 10

A Strange Greek Word
Seals the Deal

*Perhaps more than any other passage of Scripture,
I Timothy 2:11-12 has been used to restrict and limit the ministry of
women in the church. It is therefore vital that we get it right.*

Eddie Hyatt

The word "authority" in I Timothy 2:11-12 is a translation of the Greek word *authentein*, which is found only here in the entire New Testament. The very fact that it is used only here should cause one to give pause and question why that would be the case. It certainly indicates that Paul is not addressing the normal exercise of authority in the church.

A Unique Situation in Ephesus
Called for the Use of this Strange Word

If Paul was addressing the normal exercise of "authority" in the church, he would have used the Greek word *exousia*, which he and other New Testament writers use over 100 times. That Paul uses this strange Greek word that neither he nor any other New Testament writer ever uses is a clear sign that he is addressing a unique and local situation in Ephesus, and is not giving instructions for all churches everywhere.

Since the word *authentein* is used only here in the New Testament, it has been necessary to examine ancient Greek literature to see how it was used. Its use from around 600 B.C. up to the time of Paul carried the meaning of "gaining the upper hand" with connotations of control, dominance and even violence. In one case, it was used of a murder. The murderer was said to have committed *authentein* against the victim.

From around the time of Paul and onward, *authentein* begins to take on a new meaning. Although the original meaning persists, it is now also used to refer to someone who claims to be the author or originator of someone or something. In fact, our words "author" and "authentic" are derived from *authentein*.[26] But why would Paul use such a word in this passage?

The Cultural Setting

The answer is to be found in the cultural climate of Ephesus and the kind of false teaching that Timothy is confronting. We know from Acts 19:23-41 that Ephesus was the center for the worship of the female goddess known as Artemis, or Diana. As mentioned earlier, her temple, considered one of the wonders of the ancient world, was in Ephesus. Religious pilgrims came from all over the Roman world to worship at her shrine, and her presence dominated Ephesian culture.

To understand Paul's uses of *authentein*, it is important to remember that Artemis was a fertility goddess and could produce offspring without the help of a male cohort. She was totally self-sufficient. According to one ancient source, the legendary female warriors, known as the Amazons, originated from Ephesus and Artemis was their role model. Like Artemis, they did not need a man.

There is strong evidence that, in Ephesus, stories of Artemis were being mingled with Biblical stories and the gospel itself. This combining of different beliefs is called "syncretism" and is a problem in the church today. For example, a recent headline in the Dallas Morning News read, "One Part Jesus and Two Parts Buddha." The writer then explained that a growing trend in America is for people to concoct their own religion, drawing what they like from the various religions of the world and discarding what they don't like.

This sort of syncretism could more easily happen in the ancient world since there were no rapid duplication processes of either print or voice. The only thing Paul could leave with the people where he preached was the memory of what he had said and how he had behaved.

Syncretism could easily occur as people combined what they heard from Paul with the myths and legends that were a part of their local life and culture. Modern archaeology has uncovered evidence indicating that this is precisely what was happening and was the reason for Paul writing I Timothy.

Syncretism in Ephesus

Archeologists have discovered ancient Gnostic accounts of creation that have obviously combined myths from the worship of Artemis with the Genesis story of creation. These stories were probably circulating in Ephesus at the time of Paul and they certainly give a context for his statements in 2:11-12.

In each of these accounts, Eve is pictured as the instructor of Adam and the one who gives him life. In one account, Adam even refers to Eve as his mother, which is how Artemis was addressed by her devotees.

> The spirit-filled woman came to him and spoke with him saying, "Arise, Adam." And when he saw her, he said, "You are the one who has given me life. You will be called 'the mother of the living,' because she is my mother, she is the female healer, and the wife and the one who gave birth."[27]

In another account, the same ability of Artemis to give birth without the help of a male is ascribed to Eve.

> For Eve is the first virgin, the one who had no husband and yet gave birth. She is the one who acted as a physical-midwife to herself.[28]

There are other examples, but these are sufficient to show how ancient myths became entangled with Biblical truth. Without the benefit of modern recording and duplication technology, the gospel and Biblical stories, such as the creation, were spread by word of mouth--by being told and re-told. In such a setting it is easy to see how this sort of syncretism could occur as Biblical stories became entangled with local myths and legends.

Identifying the False Doctrine in Ephesus

So why does Paul use this strange Greek verb? The evidence indicates that there was a radical matriarchal movement in the church in Ephesus, actually rooted in the worship of Artemis. The erring Christian leaders had gone too far in trying to make the gospel culturally relative. They proclaimed Eve (woman) to be the author or originator of Adam (man), giving primacy to the female as was done in the worship of the mother goddess.

This became the basis for claiming primacy for the female in all of areas of life. It also became the basis for some women rejecting men and marriage because they, like Artemis, did not need a man. This is the basis for understanding Paul's statement in I Timothy 5:14-15,

> *Therefore, I desire the younger widows to marry, bear children, mange the house, give no opportunity for the adversary to speak reproachfully. For some have already turned aside to Satan.*

Summary

So, what Paul is saying in I Timothy 2:11-12 is that he does not permit a woman to teach that she is the *authentein*--the author or originator--of man. He uses the word *authentein*, not only because of the content of the false teaching, but because of the controlling, domineering manner in which it is being pushed by its proponents.

He does not use the normal word for authority, *exousia*, because he is not addressing the normal exercise of authority in the Church. He is addressing the specific problem that exists in Ephesus.

Authentein was the appropriate word for confronting the false teaching in Ephesus. That it was not appropriate for any other situation that Paul faced, is confirmed by the fact that he never used it again. Its use here also explains I Timothy 2:13-15 where Paul is simply seeking to set straight the Genesis account of creation that had been distorted by the false teachers.

After many years of researching and teaching I Timothy as part of the "Pastoral Epistles," I am convinced that Paul is here addressing a unique situation in Ephesus and never intended what he said to be applied across the board to all women and all churches everywhere.

Why We Must Get it Right

It is important that we get this right because we live in a time when the Spirit is being poured out and thousands of women are being awakened in a new way.

Dr. Susan Hyatt

For Paul, the equality of women with men was not a "woman issue," but an essential part of the gospel itself. In a similar way, I have not written this book to merely address a "woman issue," for the matter of the equality of women with men in Christ is both a church issue and an issue of world evangelism of utmost importance.

A Personal Awakening

This was made very real to me in 2009 when I had an experience that awakened me to the serious implications of teaching and living the message of gender equality in Christ. Sue had completed her doctoral dissertation on this matter several years before and had published her book, *In the Spirit We're Equal*. I was supportive, but not really committed.

On this particular morning I found found myself wide awake around 3 A.M. Not wanting to awaken Sue, I went into an adjoining room where moonlight streaming through a window added a sense of tranquility to the setting. There I sat on a sofa enjoying the quietness and solitude as I thought on the things of God and quietly prayed.

As I quietly communed with the Lord, I heard the Holy Spirit speak in my heart, perhaps as clear as I have ever heard Him speak. He said, "I want you to be more identified with Sue in what she is doing." There was a quiet pause in my heart and then I heard words that astounded me. I heard, "This message has the power to begin a mass movement from Islam to Christianity beginning with the women."

As I sat and pondered what I had just heard, I knew I was experiencing a life-altering visitation from the Lord. Almost immediately I recalled hearing an African woman—a former Muslim—being interviewed on TV. She told how she had run away from her home in Somalia at a very young age after her Muslim father had arranged for her to be married to a Muslim man in Canada.

She found her way to Europe and the Netherlands where she received an education and was elected to the Dutch Parliament. She also became a very vocal critic of Islam. I recalled the fact that instead of becoming a Christian, she had chosen to become a secularist.

As I thought on this, I realized the probable reason for her not becoming a Christian upon leaving Islam. Why would she exchange a hard form of patriarchy in Islam for a softer form of patriarchy in evangelical Christianity? In both cases she would be required to be under the authority of a male, and after her experience in Islam, that would hold no attraction to her.

If, however, she had heard the message of the woman's equal acceptance in Christ, and what Paul really taught, it could have been a completely different story. Remembering her story that morning confirmed to me the vital importance of the church understanding and preaching the woman's full redemption in Christ.

A Key to Church Growth

In 1988 I witnessed firsthand what can happen when the church dispenses with gender-determined roles and gives its members equal access based on their gifts and callings. I spent one week in Seoul, S. Korea observing the ministry of the largest church in the world at the time, founded by a woman, Choi Ja-shil, and her son-in-law, David Yonggi Cho.

At that time, the Yoido Full Gospel Church had over 600,000 members and was growing at the rate of 13,000 per month. Ninety per cent of those new members were entering the church through the 50,000 small, cell groups that met weekly in homes and offices throughout the city.

I discovered that of the 50,000 cell groups that were bringing in 90% of the growth, 48,000 were led by women. I looked at the pastoral staff of this massive congregation and discovered that of the approximate 600 pastors, two-thirds were women. I realized that without the active participation of women, this world-renowned church would shrink into a much smaller and insignificant congregation.

During this same time, a friend, Ed Lindgren, spent six weeks in Seoul studying the church growth methods of this church. After returning home to America, he wrote a manuscript entitled, *Cho's Secret Weapon--Women*.

Cho, now retired, has said that in teaching church growth to pastors all over the world, he tells them that he could never have built such a church without the full participation of women. In spite of this, he says there is still much resistance to this part of his message.

A Key for Revival

In her book, *In the Spirit We're Equal*, Sue has shown how that revival movements in history have always lifted the status of women. This happens because in revival the criterion for ministry is the presence and power of the Holy Spirit in one's life rather than factors such as education and gender.

In the 18th century Methodist revival, John Wesley was challenged when God began to raise up and anoint uneducated men and women to proclaim the gospel. At first he resisted but finally yielded himself to the fact that God was calling and sending forth both men and women even though they were not graduates of Oxford or ordained with the Church of England as was he.

He came to realize that the authority to minister is rooted in one's possession of a divine call or gift, and that ordination is simply the church's recognition of that gift. When challenged as to why he gave recognition to women preachers, he replied, "Because God owns them in the conversion of sinners, and who am I that I should withstand God."

We Must Open Ourselves to the Spirit

Much of the church still refuses to recognize the gifts of its female members and has, thereby, violated Paul's command in I Thessalonians 5:19 *not to quench the Spirit*. As a result of this disobedience, many gifts have lain dormant while millions have perished without Christ and the church has languished in defeat.

If we want to see genuine revival and world evangelism in this generation, we must dispense with our traditions and interpretations that have served to muzzle and hobble at least half the members of Christ's body. If we will move from gender-determined roles to an openness to the Spirit that recognizes His work in both men and women, we could well see the greatest Spiritual awakening and missionary movement the church has yet known.

Paul, I am sure, would approve!

Endnotes

[1] Elisabeth Schussler Fiorenza, *In Memory of Her* (New York: Crossroad, 19840, 63.

[2] "Meet Paul the apostle: trainer of misogynists," http://thesecularparent.com/meet-paul-the-apostle-trainer-of-misogynists/

[3] F. F. Bruce, *Paul: Apostle of the Heart Set Free* (Grand Rapids: Eerdmans, 1977), 15.

[4] John Chrysostom, "The Homilies of St. John Chrysostom," *Nicene and Post-Nicene Fathers*, Series I, 11:555; Eerdmans, 1956). 35.

[5] N. Clayton Croy, "A Case Study in Translators' Bias," *Priscilla Papers* (Spring 2001): 9.

[6] James G. D. Dunn, vol. 38B of *Word Biblical Commentary* (Dallas: Word Books), 894.

[7] F. C. Grant, *Hellenistic Religions: The Age of Syncretism* (New York: Liberal Arts Press, n.d.), 33.

[8] David Aune, *Prophecy in Early Christianity and the Ancient Mediterranean World* (Grand Rapids: Eerdmans, 1983), 33, 354.

[9] Susan Hyatt, *In the Spirit We're Equal* (Dallas: Hyatt Press, 1998), 39-47.

[10] Ben Witherington III, *The Paul Quest* (Downers Grove, InterVarsity Press, 1998), 220.

[11] Gordon Fee, *The First Epistle to the Corinthians* (Grand Rapids: Eerdmans, 1987), 699-708.

[12] See chapter 47 of Grudem's Systematic Theology.

[13] Fee, *The First Epistle to the Corinthians*, 704.

[14] Loren Cunningham and David J. Hamilton, *Why Not Women* (Seattle: YWAM, 2000). 190.

[15] Gilbert Bilezikian, *Beyond Sex Roles* (Grand Rapids: Baker, 1985), 288.

[16] C. K. Barrett, *The First Epistle to the Corinthians* (San Francisco: Harper & Row, 1968), 154.

[17] Fee, *The First Epistle to the Corinthians*, 269.

[18] Fee, *The First Epistle to the Corinthians*, 270.

[19] William F. Arndt and F. Wilbur Gingrich, trans., *A Greek-English Lexicon of the New Testament and Other Early Christian Literature* (Univ. of Chicago Press, 1957), 856. See also Michael W. Holmes, *The Apostolic Fathers* (Grand Rapids: Baker, 1989), 129.

[20] Susan Hyatt, *In the Spirit We're Equal* (Dallas: Hyatt Press, 1998), 256.

[21] Hyatt, *In the Spirit We're Equal*, 256-57.

[22] Berkeley & Alvera Mickelsen, "The Head of the Epistles," *Christianity Today* 25, Feb. 20, 1981.

[23] Scherman, Rabbi Nosson and Rabbi Meir Zlotowitz, eds., *The Chumash, The Stone Edition* (Brooklyn: Meśorah Publ., 1993), 14.

[24] Gordon D. Fee, *1 and 2 Timothy, Titus* (Peabody, MA: Hendrickson, 1988), 8.

[25] See the discussion in Kroeger, Catherine Clark and Mary J. Evans, eds., *The IVP Women's Bible Commentary* (Downers Grove: InterVarsity Press, 2002), 738.

[26] Craig Keener, *The IVP Bible Background Commentary: New Testament* (Downers Grove: IV Press, 1993), 611.

[27] For an exhaustive treatment of this, see Kroeger, Richard Clark and Catherine Clark Kroeger, *I Suffer Not A Woman: Rethinking 1 Timothy 2:11-15 in Light of Ancient Evidence*. Grand Rapids: Baker, 1992.

[28] Kroeger, *I Suffer Not A Woman*, 121.

[29] Kroeger, *I Suffer Not A Woman: Rethinking 1 Timothy 2:11-15 in Light of Ancient Evidence*, 121.

Selected Bibliography

Bilezikian, Gilbert. *Beyond Sex Roles* (Grand Rapids: Baker, 1985.

Bruce, F.F. *Paul: Apostle of the Heart Set Free*. Grand Rapids: Eerdmans, 1977.

Cunningham, Loren and David J. Hamilton, *Why Not Women*. Seattle: YWAM, 2000.

Fee, Gordon. *The First Epistle to the Corinthians*. Grand Rapids: Eerdmans, 1987.

Hyatt, Susan. *In the Spirit We're Equal*. Dallas: Hyatt Press, 1998.

___. *Ten Things Jesus Taught About Women*. Grapevine, TX: Hyatt Press, 213.

Keener, Craig. *The IVP Bible Background Commentary: New Testament*. Downers Grove: IV Press, 1993.

Kroeger, Richard Clark and Catherine Clark Kroeger. *I Suffer Not A Woman*. Grand Rapids: Baker, 1992.

Kroeger, Catherine and James R. Beck, Eds. *Women, Abuse and the Bible*. Grand Rapids: Baker, 1996.

Kroeger, Catherine Clark and Mary J. Evans, Eds. *The IVP Women's Bible Commentary*. Downers Grove: InterVarsity Press, 2002.

Mickelsen, Alvera, Ed. *Women, Authority and the Bible*. NP: IVP Books, 1986.

Mickelsen, Berkeley and Alvera. "The Head of the Epistles," *Christianity Today* 25, Feb. 20, 1981.

Witherington, Ben III. *The Paul Quest* (Downers Grove: InterVarsity Press, 1998.